Writing Passion
A Catullus Reader

Teacher's Guide

Ronnie Ancona

Bolchazy-Carducci Publishers, Inc.
Wauconda, Illinois USA

In-House Editor
Laurie Haight Keenan

Contributing Editor
James Chochola

Typography, Page and Cover Design
Adam Phillip Velez

Latin Text
D. F. S. Thomson
Catullus: Edited with a Textual and Interpretative Commentary
University of Toronto Press 1997
Reprinted with permission of University of Toronto Press

Cover illustration
Pablo Picasso, *Girl Reading at a Table, 1934.*
© 2004 Estate of Pablo Picasso / Artists Rights Society (ARS), New York.
The Metropolitan Museum of Art, Bequest of Florene M. Schoenborn,
in honor of William S. Lieberman, 1995 (1996.403.1)
Photograph © 1996 The Metropolitan Museum of Art.

Writing Passion: A Catullus Reader
Teacher's Guide
by Ronnie Ancona

Bolchazy-Carducci Publishers, Inc.
1000 Brown Street
Wauconda, IL 60084 USA
www.bolchazy.com

Printed in the United States of America
2005
by Publishers Graphics

ISBN 0-86516-483-5

CONTENTS

PREFACE

The purpose of this Teacher's Guide to *Writing Passion: A Catullus Reader* is to provide the Latin teacher with some additional information and resources that may facilitate the teaching of the Catullus poems included in the Student Text. Rather than repeat myself, I include here in the preface only material that is not available in the Student Text. The teacher interested in the rationale behind the Student Text or in my particular approach to the teaching of Catullus should consult the Preface and Introduction to the Student Text where these issues are addressed.

The Teacher's Guide is comprised of five sections: an enlarged text of the poems, translations of the poems, tests, discussion questions, and an annotated bibliography.

The enlarged version of the Latin poems is included so that the teacher may reproduce the poems for various pedagogical purposes, including the making of overhead transparencies, and in-class testing and review. The Latin text is reprinted with the permission of University of Toronto Press. I would like to thank Walter Brooker, Permissions Manager of University of Toronto Press, for his assistance. The text is that of D. F. S. Thomson, *Catullus: Edited with a Textual and Interpretative Commentary* (1997) except in Poem 116, line 4, where I print a comma instead of a period. Advanced Placement Latin teachers should consult the *Oxford Classical Text of Catullus* by R. Mynors (1958 or later reprints) to note where Mynors differs from Thomson, since the OCT is the text used for the Advanced Placement Examination.

The translations, which were written to be literal rather than "literary," may be used by the teacher in a number of ways: for checking his or her own sense of the Latin (the beginning teacher of Catullus, especially, may find this of use), for discussing with students different ways of translating (the more literal vs. the less literal seen in many published translations) as well as the "untranslatability" of Catullus (by showing ways in which the particular English words and constructions I have chosen are "inadequate" to the Latin). Finally, some teachers may find the translations useful to help students review their own translations. I would like to thank Oxford University Press for permission to use here my slightly revised translations of Poems 11 and 51, both taken from "The Untouched Self: Sapphic and Catullan Muses in Horace *Odes* 1.22," in *Cultivating the Muse: Struggles for Power and Inspiration in Classical Literature*. ed. Efrossini Spentzou and Don Fowler, Oxford: Oxford University Press, 2002.

The discussion questions focus on the individual poems themselves as well as on ways in which elements in one Catullus poem may connect with those in another. Mention is made of some poems that lie outside the selections in the Student Text in the hope that this may encourage both teacher and student to venture further in their reading. Teachers may find the questions useful for sparking class discussion or as topics for student papers.

The test material included (both short answer and essay) is meant to reflect the kinds of questions that students will encounter when taking the Catullus portion of the Advanced Placement* Examination in Latin Literature. Of course teachers will have their own objectives and their own distinctive interests in testing. Therefore, it is hoped that teachers will view the test material included here not as some kind of ideal, but rather as good preparation for the particular kind of exam that many of their students will be taking. Those teachers using the Student Text at the college level or in non-AP* classes at the high school level may also find the material useful as a way of checking their students on specifics of Latin forms, constructions, figures, meter etc. as well as on issues of style and interpretation.

The major difference between the bibliography in the Teacher's Guide and that found in the Student Text is the inclusion of some annotation. While I consider it vital to expose students at both the college and the high school level to scholarship on Catullus, I thought it would be most useful to reserve any comments on the sources for the Teacher's Guide. My assumption is that the teacher will have his or her own reasons for recommending various sources to students and I have no desire to interfere in that process. For the busy teacher, though, I thought some commentary would be useful, to guide him or her more quickly to material of interest. I do not comment on every source, but rather comment only when I have something to say that I think would be useful.

A few words to the teacher just beginning to teach this material. Remember, you are the key to making this material exciting for the student. The most important task as you begin is to become as comfortable as possible with the Latin you are teaching. The first time you teach this material you may find that just reading the Latin, using the notes in the Student Text, and occasionally consulting a commentary for more information than you find in the Student Text will take all of the time you have to prepare for your course. That is fine. The sense of adventure you will bring to teaching this material for the first time will be transmitted to your students. Your first responsibility is to be an adequate resource for their basic Latin needs. Then, as you have time and interest, gradually start browsing through some of the scholarship on Catullus. I think you will find some of it can add considerably to your capacity to discuss Catullus with your students.

The length of the bibliography is not meant to discourage teachers, but rather to provide a resource from which each teacher can pick and choose what might be of interest and what might be useful. While it is my hope that all teachers will find something of value in the Guide to facilitate their teaching of Catullus, it is the teacher's own excitement about the material that will likely make more of a difference to the student in the long run than anything I might have to offer here.

Finally, a word of thanks for their helpful comments to the anonymous readers of both the Student Text and the Teacher's Guide for Bolchazy-Carducci Publishers, and to Adam Velez for his design work, especially on the Student Text cover.

January, 2004

---

* AP is a registered trademark of the College Entrance Examination Board, which was not involved in the production of, and does not endorse, this product.

Large Format
Text of Poems

CATULLUS 1

Cui dono lepidum novum libellum
arida modo pumice expolitum?
Corneli, tibi: namque tu solebas
meas esse aliquid putare nugas
iam tum, cum ausus es unus Italorum   5
omne aevum tribus explicare cartis
doctis, Iuppiter, et laboriosis.
quare habe tibi quidquid hoc libelli,
qualecumque quod, <o> patrona virgo,
plus uno maneat perenne saeclo.   10

CATULLUS 2

Passer, deliciae meae puellae,
quicum ludere, quem in sinu tenere,
cui primum digitum dare appetenti
et acris solet incitare morsus,
cum desiderio meo nitenti   5
carum nescioquid lubet iocari,
ut solaciolum sui doloris,
credo, ut tum gravis acquiescat ardor;
tecum ludere sicut ipsa possem
et tristis animi levare curas!   10

CATULLUS 3

Lugete, o Veneres Cupidinesque
et quantum est hominum venustiorum:
passer mortuus est meae puellae,
passer, deliciae meae puellae,
quem plus illa oculis suis amabat.   5
nam mellitus erat suamque norat
ipsam tam bene quam puella matrem,
nec sese a gremio illius movebat,
sed circumsiliens modo huc modo illuc
ad solam dominam usque pipiabat;   10
qui nunc it per iter tenebricosum
illuc, unde negant redire quemquam.
at vobis male sit, malae tenebrae
Orci, quae omnia bella devoratis:
tam bellum mihi passerem abstulistis   15
(o factum male! o miselle passer!);
vestra nunc opera meae puellae
flendo turgiduli rubent ocelli.

Catullus 4

Phaselus ille, quem videtis, hospites,
ait fuisse navium celerrimus,
neque ullius natantis impetum trabis
nequisse praeterire, sive palmulis
opus foret volare sive linteo. 5
et hoc negat minacis Hadriatici
negare litus insulasve Cycladas
Rhodumque nobilem horridamque Thracia
Propontida trucemve Ponticum sinum,
ubi iste post phaselus antea fuit 10
comata silva; nam Cytorio in iugo
loquente saepe sibilum edidit coma.
Amastri Pontica et Cytore buxifer,
tibi haec fuisse et esse cognitissima
ait phaselus: ultima ex origine 15
tuo stetisse dicit in cacumine,
tuo imbuisse palmulas in aequore,
et inde tot per impotentia freta
erum tulisse, laeva sive dextera
vocaret aura, sive utrumque Iuppiter 20

simul secundus incidisset in pedem;

neque ulla vota litoralibus deis

sibi esse facta, cum veniret a mari

novissime hunc ad usque limpidum lacum.

sed haec prius fuere: nunc recondita　　　　　25

senet quiete seque dedicat tibi,

gemelle Castor et gemelle Castoris.

CATULLUS 5

Vivamus, mea Lesbia, atque amemus,
rumoresque senum severiorum
omnes unius aestimemus assis!
soles occidere et redire possunt;
nobis, cum semel occidit brevis lux, 5
nox est perpetua una dormienda.
da mi basia mille, deinde centum,
dein mille altera, dein secunda centum,
deinde usque altera mille, deinde centum;
dein, cum milia multa fecerimus, 10
conturbabimus, illa ne sciamus,
aut ne quis malus invidere possit
cum tantum sciat esse basiorum.

CATULLUS 7

Quaeris quot mihi basiationes
tuae, Lesbia, sint satis superque.
quam magnus numerus Libyssae harenae
lasarpiciferis iacet Cyrenis
oraclum Iovis inter aestuosi   5
et Batti veteris sacrum sepulcrum,
aut quam sidera multa, cum tacet nox,
furtivos hominum vident amores;
tam te basia multa basiare
vesano satis et super Catullo est,   10
quae nec pernumerare curiosi
possint nec mala fascinare lingua.

CATULLUS 8

Miser Catulle, desinas ineptire,
et quod vides perisse perditum ducas.
fulsere quondam candidi tibi soles,
cum ventitabas quo puella ducebat
amata nobis quantum amabitur nulla. 5
ibi illa multa cum iocosa fiebant,
quae tu volebas nec puella nolebat,
fulsere vere candidi tibi soles.
nunc iam illa non vult; tu quoque inpote<ns noli>,
nec quae fugit sectare, nec miser vive, 10
sed obstinata mente perfer, obdura.
vale, puella. iam Catullus obdurat,
nec te requiret nec rogabit invitam.
at tu dolebis, cum rogaberis nulla.
scelesta, vae te! quae tibi manet vita? 15
quis nunc te adibit? cui videberis bella?
quem nunc amabis? cuius esse diceris?
quem basiabis? cui labella mordebis?
at tu, Catulle, destinatus obdura.

CATULLUS 10

Varus me meus ad suos amores

visum duxerat e foro otiosum,

scortillum, ut mihi tum repente visum est,

non sane illepidum neque invenustum.

huc ut venimus, incidere nobis   5

sermones varii: in quibus, quid esset

iam Bithynia; quo modo se haberet;

ecquonam mihi profuisset aere.

respondi, id quod erat, nihil neque ipsis

nec praetoribus esse nec cohorti,   10

cur quisquam caput unctius referret,

praesertim quibus esset irrumator

praetor, nec faceret pili cohortem.

"at certe tamen," inquiunt "quod illic

natum dicitur esse, comparasti   15

ad lecticam homines." ego, ut puellae

unum me facerem beatiorem,

"non" inquam "mihi tam fuit maligne,

ut, provincia quod mala incidisset,

non possem octo homines parare rectos."   20

at mi nullus erat nec hic neque illic,
fractum qui veteris pedem grabati
in collo sibi collocare posset.
hic illa, ut decuit cinaediorem,
"quaeso" inquit mihi, "mi Catulle, paulum 25
istos commoda; nam volo ad Serapim
deferri." "mane," inquii puellae,
"istud quod modo dixeram me habere,
fugit me ratio: meus sodalis—
Cinna est Gaius—is sibi paravit. 30
verum, utrum illius an mei, quid ad me?
utor tam bene quam mihi pararim.
sed tu insulsa male et molesta vivis,
per quam non licet esse neglegentem."

CATULLUS 11

Furi et Aureli, comites Catulli,
sive in extremos penetrabit Indos,
litus ut longe resonante Eoa
   tunditur unda,

sive in Hyrcanos Arabasve molles,   5
seu Sagas sagittiferosve Parthos,
sive quae septemgeminus colorat
   aequora Nilus,

sive trans altas gradietur Alpes,
Caesaris visens monimenta magni,   10
Gallicum Rhenum horribile aequor ulti-
   mosque Britannos,

omnia haec, quaecumque feret voluntas
caelitum, temptare simul parati,
pauca nuntiate meae puellae   15
   non bona dicta.

cum suis vivat valeatque moechis,
quos simul complexa tenet trecentos,
nullum amans vere, sed identidem omnium
   ilia rumpens; 20

nec meum respectet, ut ante, amorem,
qui illius culpa cecidit velut prati
ultimi flos, praetereunte postquam
   tactus aratro est.

Catullus 12

Marrucine Asini, manu sinistra
non belle uteris: in ioco atque vino
tollis lintea neglegentiorum.
hoc salsum esse putas? fugit te, inepte;
quamvis sordida res et invenusta est.   5
non credis mihi? crede Pollioni
fratri, qui tua furta vel talento
mutari velit: est enim leporum
differtus puer ac facetiarum.
quare aut hendecasyllabos trecentos   10
exspecta, aut mihi linteum remitte,
quod me non movet aestimatione,
verum est mnemosynum mei sodalis.
nam sudaria Saetaba ex Hiberis
miserunt mihi muneri Fabullus   15
et Veranius; haec amem necesse est
ut Veraniolum meum et Fabullum.

CATULLUS 13

Cenabis bene, mi Fabulle, apud me
paucis, si tibi di favent, diebus,
si tecum attuleris bonam atque magnam
cenam, non sine candida puella
et vino et sale et omnibus cachinnis. 5
haec si, inquam, attuleris, venuste noster,
cenabis bene—nam tui Catulli
plenus sacculus est aranearum.
sed contra accipies meros amores
seu quid suavius elegantiusve est: 10
nam unguentum dabo quod meae puellae
donarunt Veneres Cupidinesque,
quod tu cum olfacies, deos rogabis
totum ut te faciant, Fabulle, nasum.

CATULLUS 14a (numbered as 14 in Thomson)

Ni te plus oculis meis amarem,
iucundissime Calve, munere isto
odissem te odio Vatiniano:
nam quid feci ego quidve sum locutus,
cur me tot male perderes poetis?   5
isti di mala multa dent clienti,
qui tantum tibi misit impiorum.
quod si, ut suspicor, hoc novum ac repertum
munus dat tibi Sulla litterator,
non est mi male, sed bene ac beate,   10
quod non dispereunt tui labores.
di magni, horribilem et sacrum libellum!
quem tu scilicet ad tuum Catullum
misti continuo, ut die periret
Saturnalibus optimo dierum!   15
non non hoc tibi, salse, sic abibit.
nam, si luxerit, ad librariorum
curram scrinia; Caesios, Aquinos,
Suffenum, omnia colligam venena,
ac te his suppliciis remunerabor.   20

vos hinc interea valete abite

illuc, unde malum pedem attulistis,

saecli incommoda, pessimi poetae.

CATULLUS 22

Suffenus iste, Vare, quem probe nosti,
homo est venustus et dicax et urbanus,
idemque longe plurimos facit versus.
puto esse ego illi milia aut decem aut plura
perscripta, nec sic ut fit in palimpsesto   5
relata: cartae regiae novae libri,
novi umbilici, lora rubra, membranae,
derecta plumbo et pumice omnia aequata.
haec cum legas tu, bellus ille et urbanus
Suffenus unus caprimulgus aut fossor   10
rursus videtur: tantum abhorret ac mutat.
hoc quid putemus esse? qui modo scurra
aut siquid hac re scitius videbatur,
idem inficeto est inficetior rure,
simul poemata attigit, neque idem umquam   15
aeque est beatus ac poema cum scribit:
tam gaudet in se tamque se ipse miratur.
nimirum idem omnes fallimur, neque est quisquam
quem non in aliqua re videre Suffenum
possis. suus cuique attributus est error;   20
sed non videmus manticae quod in tergo est.

CATULLUS 30

Alfene immemor atque unanimis false sodalibus,
iam te nil miseret, dure, tui dulcis amiculi?
iam me prodere, iam non dubitas fallere, perfide?
nec facta impia fallacum hominum caelicolis placent.
quae tu neglegis ac me miserum deseris in malis.   5
eheu quid faciant, dic, homines cuive habeant fidem?
certe tute iubebas animam tradere, inique, <me>
inducens in amorem, quasi tuta omnia mi forent.
idem nunc retrahis te ac tua dicta omnia factaque
ventos irrita ferre ac nebulas aerias sinis.   10
si tu oblitus es, at di meminerunt, meminit Fides,
quae te ut paeniteat postmodo facti faciet tui.

Catullus 31

Paene insularum, Sirmio, insularumque
ocelle, quascumque in liquentibus stagnis
marique vasto fert uterque Neptunus,
quam te libenter quamque laetus inviso,
vix mi ipse credens Thyniam atque Bithynos   5
liquisse campos et videre te in tuto.
o quid solutis est beatius curis,
cum mens onus reponit, ac peregrino
labore fessi venimus larem ad nostrum,
desideratoque acquiescimus lecto?   10
hoc est quod unum est pro laboribus tantis.
salve, o venusta Sirmio, atque ero gaude
gaudente, vosque lucidae lacus undae
ridete quidquid est domi cachinnorum.

Catullus 35

Poetae tenero, meo sodali,
velim Caecilio, papyre, dicas
Veronam veniat, Novi relinquens
Comi moenia Lariumque litus:
nam quasdam volo cogitationes   5
amici accipiat sui meique.
quare, si sapiet, viam vorabit,
quamvis candida milies puella
euntem revocet, manusque collo
ambas iniciens roget morari.   10
quae nunc, si mihi vera nuntiantur,
illum deperit impotente amore:
nam quo tempore legit incohatam
Dindymi dominam, ex eo misellae
ignes interiorem edunt medullam.   15
ignosco tibi, Sapphica puella
musa doctior: est enim venuste
Magna Caecilio incohata Mater.

Catullus 36

Annales Volusi, cacata carta,
votum solvite pro mea puella.
nam sanctae Veneri Cupidinique
vovit, si sibi restitutus essem
desissemque truces vibrare iambos,   5
electissima pessimi poetae
scripta tardipedi deo daturam
infelicibus ustulanda lignis,
et hoc pessima se puella vidit
iocose lepide vovere divis.   10
nunc, o caeruleo creata ponto,
quae sanctum Idalium Uriosque apertos
quaeque Ancona Cnidumque harundinosam
colis quaeque Amathunta quaeque Golgos
quaeque Dyrrachium Hadriae tabernam,   15
acceptum face redditumque votum,
si non illepidum neque invenustum est.
at vos interea venite in ignem,
pleni ruris et inficetiarum
annales Volusi, cacata carta.   20

CATULLUS 40

Quaenam te mala mens, miselle Raude,
agit praecipitem in meos iambos?
quis deus tibi non bene advocatus
vecordem parat excitare rixam?
an ut pervenias in ora vulgi? 5
quid vis? qualubet esse notus optas?
eris, quandoquidem meos amores
cum longa voluisti amare poena.

Catullus 43

Salve, nec minimo puella naso
nec bello pede nec nigris ocellis
nec longis digitis nec ore sicco
nec sane nimis elegante lingua.
decoctoris amica Formiani,   5
ten provincia narrat esse bellam?
tecum Lesbia nostra comparatur?
o saeclum insipiens et inficetum!

CATULLUS 44

O funde noster seu Sabine seu Tiburs
(nam te esse Tiburtem autumant, quibus non est
cordi Catullum laedere; at quibus cordi est,
quovis Sabinum pignore esse contendunt),
sed seu Sabine sive verius Tiburs,   5
fui libenter in tua suburbana
villa, malamque pectore expuli tussim,
non inmerenti quam mihi meus venter,
dum sumptuosas appeto, dedit, cenas:
nam, Sestianus dum volo esse conviva,   10
orationem in Antium petitorem
plenam veneni et pestilentiae legi.
hic me gravedo frigida et frequens tussis
quassavit usque, dum in tuum sinum fugi,
et me recuravi otioque et urtica.   15
quare refectus maximas tibi grates
ago, meum quod non es ulta peccatum.
nec deprecor iam, si nefaria scripta
Sesti recepso, quin gravedinem et tussim
non mi, sed ipsi Sestio ferat frigus,   20
qui tunc vocat me, cum malum librum legi.

CATULLUS 45

Acmen Septimius suos amores
tenens in gremio "mea" inquit "Acme,
ni te perdite amo atque amare porro
omnes sum assidue paratus annos,
quantum qui pote plurimum perire,   5
solus in Libya Indiaque tosta
caesio veniam obvius leoni."
hoc ut dixit, Amor sinistra ut ante
dextra sternuit approbationem.
   at Acme leviter caput reflectens   10
et dulcis pueri ebrios ocellos
illo purpureo ore saviata,
"sic," inquit "mea vita Septimille,
huic uni domino usque serviamus,
ut multo mihi maior acriorque   15
ignis mollibus ardet in medullis."
hoc ut dixit, Amor sinistra ut ante
dextra sternuit approbationem.
   nunc ab auspicio bono profecti
mutuis animis amant amantur.   20

unam Septimius misellus Acmen
mavult quam Syrias Britanniasque:
uno in Septimio fidelis Acme
facit delicias libidinesque.
quis ullos homines beatiores 25
vidit, quis venerem auspicatiorem?

Catullus 46

Iam ver egelidos refert tepores,
iam caeli furor aequinoctialis
iucundis Zephyri silescit auris.
linquantur Phrygii, Catulle, campi
Nicaeaeque ager uber aestuosae: 5
ad claras Asiae volemus urbes.
iam mens praetrepidans avet vagari,
iam laeti studio pedes vigescunt.
o dulces comitum valete coetus,
longe quos simul a domo profectos   10
diversae varie viae reportant.

CATULLUS 49

Disertissime Romuli nepotum,
quot sunt quotque fuere, Marce Tulli,
quotque post aliis erunt in annis,
gratias tibi maximas Catullus
agit pessimus omnium poeta,   5
tanto pessimus omnium poeta
quanto tu optimus omnium patronus.

Catullus 50

Hesterno, Licini, die otiosi
multum lusimus in meis tabellis,
ut convenerat esse delicatos:
scribens versiculos uterque nostrum
ludebat numero modo hoc modo illoc,   5
reddens mutua per iocum atque vinum.
atque illinc abii tuo lepore
incensus, Licini, facetiisque,
ut nec me miserum cibus iuvaret
nec somnus tegeret quiete ocellos,   10
sed toto indomitus furore lecto
versarer, cupiens videre lucem,
ut tecum loquerer simulque ut essem.
at defessa labore membra postquam
semimortua lectulo iacebant,   15
hoc, iucunde, tibi poema feci,
ex quo perspiceres meum dolorem.
nunc audax cave sis, precesque nostras,
oramus, cave despuas, ocelle,
ne poenas Nemesis reposcat a te.   20
est vemens dea; laedere hanc caveto.

Catullus 51

Ille mi par esse deo videtur,
ille, si fas est, superare divos,
qui sedens adversus identidem te
   spectat et audit

dulce ridentem, misero quod omnis   5
eripit sensus mihi: nam simul te,
Lesbia, aspexi, nihil est super mi
   <vocis in ore>

lingua sed torpet, tenuis sub artus
flamma demanat, sonitu suopte   10
tintinant aures, gemina teguntur
   lumina nocte.

otium, Catulle, tibi molestum est;
otio exsultas nimiumque gestis;
otium et reges prius et beatas   15
   perdidit urbes.

Catullus 60

Num te leaena montibus Libystinis
aut Scylla latrans infima inguinum parte
tam mente dura procreavit ac taetra
ut supplicis vocem in novissimo casu
contemptam haberes, a nimis fero corde?   5

CATULLUS 64 (lines 50–253)

haec vestis priscis hominum variata figuris 50
heroum mira virtutes indicat arte.
namque fluentisono prospectans litore Diae
Thesea cedentem celeri cum classe tuetur
indomitos in corde gerens Ariadna furores,
necdum etiam sese quae visit visere credit, 55
utpote fallaci quae tunc primum excita somno
desertam in sola miseram se cernat harena.
immemor at iuvenis fugiens pellit vada remis,
irrita ventosae linquens promissa procellae;
quem procul ex alga maestis Minois ocellis 60
saxea ut effigies bacchantis, prospicit, eheu,
prospicit et magnis curarum fluctuat undis,
non flavo retinens subtilem vertice mitram,
non contecta levi velatum pectus amictu,
non tereti strophio lactentis vincta papillas, 65
omnia quae toto delapsa e corpore passim
ipsius ante pedes fluctus salis alludebant.
sed neque tum mitrae neque tum fluitantis amictus
illa vicem curans toto ex te pectore, Theseu,
toto animo, tota pendebat perdita mente. 70

a misera, assiduis quam luctibus externavit

spinosas Erycina serens in pectore curas,

illa tempestate, ferox qua robore Theseus

egressus curvis e litoribus Piraei

attigit iniusti regis Gortynia templa.   75

    nam perhibent olim crudeli peste coactam

Androgeoneae poenas exsolvere caedis

electos iuvenes simul et decus innuptarum

Cecropiam solitam esse dapem dare Minotauro.

quis angusta malis cum moenia vexarentur,   80

ipse suum Theseus pro caris corpus Athenis

proicere optavit potius quam talia Cretam

funera Cecropiae nec funera portarentur.

atque ita nave levi nitens ac lenibus auris

magnanimum ad Minoa venit sedesque superbas.   85

hunc simul ac cupido conspexit lumine virgo

regia, quam suavis exspirans castus odores

lectulus in molli complexu matris alebat,

quales Eurotae progignunt flumina myrtus

aurave distinctos educit verna colores,   90

non prius ex illo flagrantia declinavit

lumina, quam cuncto concepit corpore flammam

funditus atque imis exarsit tota medullis.

heu misere exagitans immiti corde furores

sancte puer, curis hominum qui gaudia misces, 95

quaeque regis Golgos quaeque Idalium frondosum,

qualibus incensam iactastis mente puellam

fluctibus, in flavo saepe hospite suspirantem!

quantos illa tulit languenti corde timores!

quam tum saepe magis fulgore expalluit auri, 100

cum saevum cupiens contra contendere monstrum

aut mortem appeteret Theseus aut praemia laudis!

non ingrata tamen frustra munuscula divis

promittens tacito succepit vota labello:

nam velut in summo quatientem brachia Tauro 105

quercum aut conigeram sudanti cortice pinum

indomitus turbo contorquens flamine robur

eruit (illa procul radicitus exturbata

prona cadit, late quaeviscumque obvia frangens),

sic domito saevum prostravit corpore Theseus 110

nequiquam vanis iactantem cornua ventis.

inde pedem sospes multa cum laude reflexit

errabunda regens tenui vestigia filo,

ne labyrintheis e flexibus egredientem

tecti frustraretur inobservabilis error. 115

    sed quid ego a primo digressus carmine plura

commemorem, ut linquens genitoris filia vultum,

ut consanguineae complexum, ut denique matris,

quae misera in gnata deperdita laeta<batur>,

omnibus his Thesei dulcem praeoptarit amorem;   120

aut ut vecta rati spumosa ad litora Diae

<venerit,> aut ut eam devinctam lumina somno

liquerit immemori discedens pectore coniunx?

saepe illam perhibent ardenti corde furentem

clarisonas imo fudisse e pectore voces,   125

ac tum praeruptos tristem conscendere montes,

unde aciem <in> pelagi vastos protenderet aestus,

tum tremuli salis adversas procurrere in undas

mollia nudatae tollentem tegmina surae,

atque haec extremis maestam dixisse querellis,   130

frigidulos udo singultus ore cientem:

"sicine me patriis avectam, perfide, ab aris,

perfide, deserto liquisti in litore, Theseu?

sicine discedens neglecto numine divum,

immemor a! devota domum periuria portas?   135

nullane res potuit crudelis flectere mentis

consilium? tibi nulla fuit clementia praesto,

immite ut nostri vellet miserescere pectus?

at non haec quondam blanda promissa dedisti

voce mihi, non haec miseram sperare iubebas,   140

sed conubia laeta, sed optatos hymenaeos,

quae cuncta aerii discerpunt irrita venti.

nunc iam nulla viro iuranti femina credat,

nulla viri speret sermones esse fideles,

quis dum aliquid cupiens animus praegestit apisci,   145

nil metuunt iurare, nihil promittere parcunt;

sed simul ac cupidae mentis satiata libido est,

dicta nihil meminere, nihil periuria curant.

certe ego te in medio versantem turbine leti

eripui, et potius germanum amittere crevi   150

quam tibi fallaci supremo in tempore dessem.

pro quo dilaceranda feris dabor alitibusque

praeda, neque iniecta tumulabor mortua terra.

quaenam te genuit sola sub rupe leaena,

quod mare conceptum spumantibus exspuit undis,   155

quae Syrtis, quae Scylla rapax, quae vasta Charybdis,

talia qui reddis pro dulci praemia vita?

si tibi non cordi fuerant conubia nostra,

saeva quod horrebas prisci praecepta parentis,

attamen in vestras potuisti ducere sedes,   160

quae tibi iucundo famularer serva labore,

candida permulcens liquidis vestigia lymphis,

purpureave tuum consternens veste cubile.

sed quid ego ignaris nequiquam conqueror auris,

exsternata malo, quae nullis sensibus auctae   165

nec missas audire queunt nec reddere voces?

ille autem prope iam mediis versatur in undis,

nec quisquam apparet vacua mortalis in alga.

sic nimis insultans extremo tempore saeva

fors etiam nostris invidit questibus auris.   170

Iuppiter omnipotens, utinam ne tempore primo

Gnosia Cecropiae tetigissent litora puppes,

indomito nec dira ferens stipendia tauro

perfidus in Creta religasset navita funem,

nec malus haec celans dulci crudelia forma   175

consilia in nostris requiesset sedibus hospes!

nam quo me referam? quali spe perdita nitor?

Idaeosne petam montes? at gurgite lato

discernens ponti truculentum dividit aequor.

an patris auxilium sperem? quemne ipsa reliqui   180

respersum iuvenem fraterna caede secuta?

coniugis an fido consoler memet amore?

quine fugit lentos incurvans gurgite remos?

praeterea nullo colitur sola insula tecto,

nec patet egressus pelagi cingentibus undis.   185

nulla fugae ratio, nulla spes: omnia muta,

omnia sunt deserta, ostentant omnia letum.

non tamen ante mihi languescent lumina morte,

nec prius a fesso secedent corpore sensus,

quam iustam a divis exposcam prodita multam 190

caelestumque fidem postrema comprecer hora.

quare facta virum multantes vindice poena

Eumenides, quibus anguino redimita capillo

frons exspirantis praeportat pectoris iras,

huc huc adventate, meas audite querellas, 195

quas ego, vae miserae, imis proferre medullis

cogor inops, ardens, amenti caeca furore.

quae quoniam verae nascuntur pectore ab imo,

vos nolite pati nostrum vanescere luctum,

sed quali solam Theseus me mente reliquit, 200

tali mente, deae, funestet seque suosque."

  has postquam maesto profudit pectore voces,

supplicium saevis exposcens anxia factis,

annuit invicto caelestum numine rector;

quo motu tellus atque horrida contremuerunt 205

aequora concussitque micantia sidera mundus.

ipse autem caeca mentem caligine Theseus

consitus oblito dimisit pectore cuncta

quae mandata prius constanti mente tenebat,

dulcia nec maesto sustollens signa parenti   210

sospitem Erectheum se ostendit visere portum.

namque ferunt olim, classi cum moenia divae

linquentem gnatum ventis concrederet Aegeus,

talia complexum iuveni mandata dedisse:

"gnate mihi longe iucundior unice vita,   215

gnate, ego quem in dubios cogor dimittere casus,

reddite in extrema nuper mihi fine senectae,

quandoquidem fortuna mea ac tua fervida virtus

eripit invito mihi te, cui languida nondum

lumina sunt gnati cara saturata figura,   220

non ego te gaudens laetanti pectore mittam,

nec te ferre sinam fortunae signa secundae,

sed primum multas expromam mente querellas,

canitiem terra atque infuso pulvere foedans;

inde infecta vago suspendam lintea malo,   225

nostros ut luctus nostraeque incendia mentis

carbasus obscurata dicet ferrugine Hibera.

quod tibi si sancti concesserit incola Itoni,

quae nostrum genus ac sedes defendere Erecthei

annuit, ut tauri respergas sanguine dextram,   230

tum vero facito ut memori tibi condita corde

haec vigeant mandata, nec ulla oblitteret aetas;
ut simul ac nostros invisent lumina collis
funestam antennae deponant undique vestem
candidaque intorti sustollant vela rudentes,   235
quam primum cernens ut laeta gaudia mente
agnoscam, cum te reducem aetas prospera sistet."
haec mandata prius constanti mente tenentem
Thesea ceu pulsae ventorum flamine nubes
aerium nivei montis liquere cacumen.   240
at pater, ut summa prospectum ex arce petebat,
anxia in assiduos absumens lumina fletus,
cum primum inflati conspexit lintea veli,
praecipitem sese scopulorum e vertice iecit,
amissum credens immiti Thesea fato.   245
sic, funesta domus ingressus tecta paterna
morte, ferox Theseus, qualem Minoidi luctum
obtulerat mente immemori, talem ipse recepit.
quae tum prospectans cedentem maesta carinam
multiplices animo volvebat saucia curas.   250
    at parte ex alia florens volitabat Iacchus
cum thiaso Satyrorum et Nysigenis Silenis,
te quaerens, Ariadna, tuoque incensus amore.

Catullus 65

Etsi me assiduo defectum cura dolore
    sevocat a doctis, Hortale, virginibus,
nec potis est dulcis Musarum expromere fetus
    mens animi, tantis fluctuat ipsa malis—
namque mei nuper Lethaeo in gurgite fratris   5
    pallidulum manans alluit unda pedem,
Troia Rhoeteo quem subter litore tellus
    ereptum nostris obterit ex oculis.

.   .   .   .

    numquam ego te, vita frater amabilior,   10
aspiciam posthac? at certe semper amabo,
    semper maesta tua carmina morte canam,
qualia sub densis ramorum concinit umbris
    Daulias, absumpti fata gemens Ityli.—
sed tamen in tantis maeroribus, Hortale, mitto   15
    haec expressa tibi carmina Battiadae,
ne tua dicta vagis nequiquam credita ventis
    effluxisse meo forte putes animo,
ut missum sponsi furtivo munere malum
    procurrit casto virginis e gremio,   20

quod miserae oblitae molli sub veste locatum,

dum adventu matris prosilit, excutitur,

atque illud prono praeceps agitur decursu,

huic manat tristi conscius ore rubor.

CATULLUS 68 (lines 1–40)

Quod mihi fortuna casuque oppressus acerbo
    conscriptum hoc lacrimis mittis epistolium,
naufragum ut eiectum spumantibus aequoris undis
    sublevem et a mortis limine restituam,
quem neque sancta Venus molli requiescere somno   5
    desertum in lecto caelibe perpetitur,
nec veterum dulci scriptorum carmine Musae
    oblectant, cum mens anxia pervigilat:
id gratum est mihi, me quoniam tibi dicis amicum,
    muneraque et Musarum hinc petis et Veneris.   10
sed tibi ne mea sint ignota incommoda, Manli,
    neu me odisse putes hospitis officium,
accipe quis merser fortunae fluctibus ipse,
    ne amplius a misero dona beata petas.
tempore quo primum vestis mihi tradita pura est,   15
    iucundum cum aetas florida ver ageret,
multa satis lusi: non est dea nescia nostri,
    quae dulcem curis miscet amaritiem.
sed totum hoc studium luctu fraterna mihi mors
    abstulit. o misero frater adempte mihi,   20

tu mea tu moriens fregisti commoda, frater,
    tecum una tota est nostra sepulta domus;
omnia tecum una perierunt gaudia nostra
    quae tuus in vita dulcis alebat amor.
cuius ego interitu tota de mente fugavi   25
    haec studia atque omnes delicias animi.
quare, quod scribis Veronae turpe Catullo
    esse, quod hic quisquis de meliore nota
frigida deserto tepefactet membra cubili,
    id, Manli, non est turpe, magis miserum est.   30
ignosces igitur si, quae mihi luctus ademit,
    haec tibi non tribuo munera, cum nequeo.
nam, quod scriptorum non magna est copia apud me,
    hoc fit, quod Romae vivimus: illa domus,
illa mihi sedes, illic mea carpitur aetas;   35
    huc una ex multis capsula me sequitur.
quod cum ita sit, nolim statuas nos mente maligna
    id facere aut animo non satis ingenuo,
quod tibi non utriusque petenti copia posta est:
    ultro ego deferrem, copia siqua foret.   40

Catullus 69

Noli admirari, quare tibi femina nulla,
    Rufe, velit tenerum supposuisse femur,
non si illam rarae labefactes munere vestis
    aut perluciduli deliciis lapidis.
laedit te quaedam mala fabula, qua tibi fertur   5
    valle sub alarum trux habitare caper.
hunc metuunt omnes, neque mirum: nam mala valde est
    bestia, nec quicum bella puella cubet.
quare aut crudelem nasorum interfice pestem,
    aut admirari desine cur fugiunt.   10

Catullus 70

Nulli se dicit mulier mea nubere malle
  quam mihi, non si se Iuppiter ipse petat.
dicit; sed mulier cupido quod dicit amanti,
  in vento et rapida scribere oportet aqua.

CATULLUS 72

Dicebas quondam solum te nosse Catullum,
    Lesbia, nec prae me velle tenere Iovem.
dilexi tum te non tantum ut vulgus amicam,
    sed pater ut gnatos diligit et generos.
nunc te cognovi; quare, etsi impensius uror,   5
    multo mi tamen es vilior et levior.
qui potis est, inquis? quod amantem iniuria talis
    cogit amare magis, sed bene velle minus.

Catullus 76

Si qua recordanti benefacta priora voluptas
    est homini, cum se cogitat esse pium,
nec sanctam violasse fidem, nec foedere in ullo
    divum ad fallendos numine abusum homines,
multa parata manent in longa aetate, Catulle,   5
    ex hoc ingrato gaudia amore tibi.
nam quaecumque homines bene cuiquam aut dicere possunt
    aut facere, haec a te dictaque factaque sunt.
omnia quae ingratae perierunt credita menti.
    quare cur tete iam amplius excrucies?   10
quin tu animo offirmas atque istinc te ipse reducis
    et dis invitis desinis esse miser?
difficile est longum subito deponere amorem,
    difficile est, verum hoc qua lubet efficias;
una salus haec est, hoc est tibi pervincendum,   15
    hoc facias, sive id non pote sive pote.
o di, si vestrum est misereri, aut si quibus umquam
    extremam iam ipsa in morte tulistis opem,
me miserum aspicite et, si vitam puriter egi,
    eripite hanc pestem perniciemque mihi,   20

quae mihi subrepens imos ut torpor in artus

    expulit ex omni pectore laetitias.

non iam illud quaero, contra ut me diligat illa,

    aut, quod non potis est, esse pudica velit:

ipse valere opto et taetrum hunc deponere morbum.   25

    o di, reddite mi hoc pro pietate mea.

CATULLUS 77

Rufe mihi frustra ac nequiquam credite amice
    (frustra? immo magno cum pretio atque malo),
sicine subrepsti mi atque intestina perurens
    ei misero eripuisti omnia nostra bona?
eripuisti, eheu nostrae crudele venenum   5
    vitae, eheu nostrae pestis amicitiae.

CATULLUS 84

Chommoda dicebat, si quando commoda vellet
    dicere, et insidias Arrius hinsidias,
et tum mirifice sperabat se esse locutum,
    cum quantum poterat dixerat hinsidias.
credo, sic mater, sic liber avunculus eius,   5
    sic maternus avus dixerat atque avia.
hoc misso in Syriam requierant omnibus aures:
    audibant eadem haec leniter et leviter,
nec sibi postilla metuebant talia verba,
    cum subito affertur nuntius horribilis,   10
Ionios fluctus, postquam illuc Arrius isset,
    iam non Ionios esse sed Hionios.

Catullus 85

Odi et amo. quare id faciam, fortasse requiris.
nescio, sed fieri sentio et excrucior.

CATULLUS 86

Quintia formosa est multis. mihi candida, longa,
    recta est: haec ego sic singula confiteor,
totum illud "formosa" nego: nam nulla venustas,
    nulla in tam magno est corpore mica salis.
Lesbia formosa est, quae cum pulcerrima tota est,   5
    tum omnibus una omnis surripuit veneres.

CATULLUS 87

Nulla potest mulier tantum se dicere amatam
   vere, quantum a me Lesbia amata mea es.
nulla fides ullo fuit umquam in foedere tanta,
   quanta in amore tuo ex parte reperta mea est.

Catullus 96

Si quicquam mutis gratum acceptumve sepulcris
    accidere a nostro, Calve, dolore potest,
quo desiderio veteres renovamus amores
    atque olim missas flemus amicitias,
certe non tanto mors immatura dolori est   5
    Quintiliae, quantum gaudet amore tuo.

CATULLUS 101

Multas per gentes et multa per aequora vectus
    advenio has miseras, frater, ad inferias,
ut te postremo donarem munere mortis
    et mutam nequiquam alloquerer cinerem,
quandoquidem fortuna mihi tete abstulit ipsum,   5
    heu miser indigne frater adempte mihi.
nunc tamen interea haec, prisco quae more parentum
    tradita sunt tristi munere ad inferias,
accipe fraterno multum manantia fletu,
    atque in perpetuum, frater, ave atque vale.   10

Catullus 109

Iucundum, mea vita, mihi proponis: amorem
    hunc nostrum inter nos perpetuum usque fore.
di magni, facite ut vere promittere possit,
    atque id sincere dicat et ex animo,
ut liceat nobis tota perducere vita   5
    aeternum hoc sanctae foedus amicitiae.

CATULLUS 116

Saepe tibi studiose, animo venante, requirens
    carmina uti possem mittere Battiadae,
qui te lenirem nobis, neu conarere
    tela infesta <meum> mittere in usque caput,
hunc video mihi nunc frustra sumptum esse laborem,   5
    Gelli, nec nostras hinc valuisse preces.
contra nos tela ista tua evitabimus acta,
    at fixus nostris tu dabis supplicium.

TRANSLATIONS OF THE POEMS

Poem 1

To whom do I present (my) new little book just now polished with dry pumice? To you, Cornelius, for you were accustomed to consider my worthless stuff something even then when you alone of (the) Italians dared to unfold all of history in three rolls, learned, Jupiter, and full of work. Therefore have for yourself whatever this is of a book, which, of whatever sort (it is), O patron virgin, may it endure lasting more than one generation.

Poem 2

Sparrow, delight of my girlfriend, with whom to play, whom to hold in her embrace, for whom, seeking, to give the tip of her finger and incite sharp bites she is accustomed, when it is pleasing to my shining object of desire/to her shining with desire for me/to play I do not know what dear thing as a little comfort for her pain, I believe, so that/with the result that/then her heavy passion may find relief; I wish I could play with you just as she herself does and relieve the sad cares of my mind.

Poem 3

Mourn, O Venuses and Cupids and how much there is/how many there are of rather charming people: my girlfriend's sparrow has died/is dead, the sparrow, my girlfriend's delight, which/whom she loved more than her own eyes. For it/he was honey-sweet and knew its/his own mistress as well as a girl (knows) her mother, nor did it/he use to move from her lap, but jumping around now this way now that way continually used to chirp to its/his mistress/owner alone; it/he who now goes through a dark journey to that place, from where they say that no one returns. But may you suffer, evil darkness of Orcus, (you) who swallow all handsome things: you have carried off from me the so handsome sparrow (o evil deed/o thing done badly! o unfortunate sparrow!); now through your doing my girlfriend's swollen little eyes become red from weeping.

Poem 4

That light ship which you see, guests/strangers, says that he was the fastest of ships, and that he was not unable to go beyond the rapid motion of any floating ship, which it was necessary to fly with oars or with a sail. And he says that the shore of the threatening Adriatic does not deny this or the Cyclades islands and noble Rhodes and Propontis, rough because of the wind from west of north or the harsh Pontic gulf, where that one, afterwards a light ship, before was a leafy forest; for on the ridge of Mount Cytorus he often put forth a whistling sound with his speaking foliage. Pontic Amastris and Mount Cytorus producing box trees, the light ship says these things were and are very (well) known to you: and he says that from his earliest starting point he stood on your peak, wet his oars in your sea, and from that point carried his master through so many wild straits, whether a breeze coming from the left or coming from the right was calling, or whether a favorable Jupiter had fallen on each sheet at the same time; and that no vows were made by him to the gods of the shore when he was coming most recently from the sea all the way to this clear lake. But these things were before: now he is old in his secluded rest and dedicates himself to you, twin Castor and twin of Castor.

Poem 5

Let us live, my Lesbia, and let us love, and let us value the gossip of rather strict old men at one penny! Suns are able to set and return; for us, when once the brief light has set, one continuing night must be slept. Give me a thousand kisses, then a hundred, then another thousand, then a second hundred, then continuously another thousand, then a hundred; then, when we (will) have done/counted up many thousands, we will mix up (the accounting)/we will go bankrupt, so that we may not know them (i.e. the kisses, how many there are), nor some hostile person be able to envy us when he knows there is so much kissing/so many kisses.

Poem 7

You ask, Lesbia, how many of your kissings are enough and more than enough for me. As great a number of Libyan sand(s) as lies in silphium-bearing Cyrene between the oracle of very hot Jupiter and the sacred tomb of ancient Battus, or as many stars, as when the night is silent, see people's secret loves; that you kiss so many kisses is enough and more than enough for crazy Catullus, so that inter-fering (people) cannot count them up nor an evil tongue bewitch.

Poem 8

Unhappy Catullus, stop playing the fool, and what you see has perished consider lost. Once radiant suns shined brightly for you, when you used to come frequently where the girl led, loved by us/me as much as no woman will be loved. Then when those many things full of fun were happening, which you used to want and the girl didn't not want, truly radiant suns shined brightly for you. Now at last she doesn't want (those things); you, also, powerless, don't want, and don't pursue the one who flees, and don't live unhappy, but with resolute mind endure, be persistent. Farewell, girl. Now Catullus is persistent, he will not try to bring you back and will not beg you unwilling. But you will suffer, when you will not be asked for at all. Wicked woman, woe to you! What life remains for you? Who now will approach you? To whom will you seem beautiful? Whom now will you love? Whose will you be said to be? Whom will you kiss? Whose lips will you bite? But you, Catullus, stubborn, persist.

Poem 10

My (friend) Varus had brought me, at leisure, from the forum to go and see his lover, a little/young tart, as it then suddenly seemed to me, not very lacking in refinement and charm. When we came here, various topics of conversation presented themselves to us: among them, what (sort of place) Bithynia was now, how it was doing, whether it had profited me with any money. I answered, that which was (the case), that there was nothing why/there was no reason why, for the people themselves or for the praetors or for the staff, anyone would bring back/render his head more oiled/would return more wealthy, especially those for whom the praetor was a bastard, and didn't value his staff a bit. "But certainly, nevertheless," they say, " you bought people for a litter/for the purpose of carrying a litter, (that) which is said to have been born there/is said to be native to there. I, in order to make myself alone more fortunate to the girl, say, "It wasn't so bad, didn't go so poorly for me that, because a bad province happened to befall me, I couldn't buy eight erect people." But I had no one neither here nor there who could place on his neck the broken leg of an old bed. At this point she, as befitted someone rather shameless said to me "Please, my (dear) Catullus, lend them to me for a short while; for I want to be carried to (the temple of) Serapis." I said to the girl, "Wait. That thing which I had just now said I have, my reason escaped me/I lost my wits: my comrade—that's Cinna, Gaius—he bought them for himself. But what is it to me whether they are his or mine? I use them as well as if I had bought them for myself. But you are/live awfully stupid(ly) and annoying(ly), according to whom it is not permitted to be careless.

Poem 11

Furius and Aurelius, companions of Catullus, whether he will penetrate into the furthest inhabitants of India, where the shore is beaten by the far resounding eastern wave, or into the Hyrcani or soft Arabs, or the Sagae and arrow-bearing Parthians, or the waters which the sevenfold Nile dyes, or he will proceed across the tall Alps, going and seeing the memorials of great Caesar, the Gallic Rhine the terrifying sea, and the furthest Britons, prepared together to attempt all these things, whatever the will of the gods will bring, tell a few not nice words to my girlfriend. Let her live and be well with her adulterers, whom, three hundred, she holds together, having embraced them, loving not one of them truly, but again and again breaking the balls of all of them; let her not await my love as before, which through her fault has fallen like a flower of the furthest part of the meadow, after it has been touched by the plough passing by.

Poem 12

Asinius Marrucinus, you use your left hand not nicely: in/amid joking and wine you take away/steal the napkins of rather careless people. Do you think this is funny? You are mistaken, fool; it's an ever so vulgar and unattractive thing. You don't believe me? Believe Pollio, your brother, who would be willing to have your thefts exchanged/undone even for a talent: for he is a boy full of grace and wit. Therefore either wait for three hundred hendecasyllables or give me back my napkin which moves me not because of its value, but is a souvenir of my companion. For Fabullus and Veranius sent me Saetaban napkins as a gift from (the land of) the Spaniards; it is necessary for me to love them as (I love) my dear Veranius and Fabullus.

Poem 13

You will dine well, my Fabullus, at my house within a few days, if the gods favor you, if you bring/ will have brought with you a good and large dinner, not without a radiant girl and wine and salt/wit and all kinds of laughter. If, I say, you bring/will have brought these things, my charming man, you will dine well—for the little money bag of your Catullus is full of cobwebs. But in return you will receive pure/unmixed love or if there is anything more pleasing or refined: for I will give you perfume which the Venuses and Cupids gave as a gift to my girlfriend, which, when you smell (it), you will ask the gods, Fabullus, to make you all nose.

Poem 14a

If I did not love you more than my eyes, most agreeable Calvus, I would hate you with the hatred of Vatinius because of that gift of yours: for what have I done or what have I said on account of which you should destroy me wickedly with so many poets? May the gods give many bad things to that client of yours who sent you so much of undutiful ones/things. But if, as I suspect, Sulla, the elementary school teacher, gives you this new and discovered/newly discovered gift, it is not bad for me, but good and fortunate, because your efforts are not being destroyed. Great gods, what a monstrous and detestable little book! You, of course, sent it to your Catullus immediately so that he would perish on the best day of days, the Saturnalia. Funny guy, this will not be allowed to pass for you in this way (i.e. you will not be allowed to get away with this in this way). For, if it has become light, I will run to the shelves of the booksellers; I will collect all the poisons, the Caesii, the Aquini, and Suffenus, and I will pay you back with these punishments. You meanwhile farewell, go away from here to that place from where you brought your bad foot, you afflictions of a lifetime, worst of poets.

Poem 22

That Suffenus of yours, Varus, whom you know well, is a charming, witty, and urbane person, and yet he writes very many verses by far/really very many verses. I think thousands, ten [thousands] or more have been fully written by him, and not, (just) as usually happens, brought back/rendered on re-cycled material: the book's splendid, new sheets of papyrus, new knobs, red leather straps, parchment covers, all marked with lead and made level with pumice. When you read these, that fine and urbane Suffenus seems to be, on the other hand, an ordinary country bumpkin or uncouth guy: he is different and changes so much. What should we think of this/think this is? The one who just now seemed to be a witty person or, if anything is more clever than this thing, the same one is more boorish than the boorish countryside, as soon as he has touched/taken up the poems, and he/the same one is never equally happy as when he is writing a poem: he delights so in himself and he, himself, so admires himself. Of course we all are deceived with respect to the same thing, nor is there anyone whom you could not see as Suffenus in some regard. To each person has been assigned his or her own delusion, but we don't see that part of the pack which is on our backs.

Poem 30

Alfenus, unmindful and false to companions sharing a single attitude, now do you pity not at all, harsh one, your sweet little friend? Faithless one, now do you not hesitate to betray me, now to deceive me? The disloyal deeds of deceptive people do not please the gods. You neglect these things and you abandon me, unhappy, in bad circumstances. Alas, tell (me), what should people do, or in whom should they have trust? You certainly used to ask me to hand over my life, treacherous one, enticing me into love, as if all things were safe for me. Now you draw yourself back and allow the winds and lofty mists to carry all your words and deeds (as) empty. If you have forgotten, still the gods remember, Fides remembers, which/who later will bring it about that you regret your action.

Poem 31

Sirmio, darling of almost islands and islands, whichever ones each Neptune carries in liquid pools and the huge sea, how gladly and how happily I see you, I myself scarcely trusting myself that I have left behind Thynia and the Bithynian fields and that I see you safely. O what is more fortunate than cares set free, when the mind puts down its burden, and tired by our work abroad we have come to our household god, and rest in our longed for bed? This is the one thing which is in return for such great labors. Hello, o charming Sirmio, and rejoice in your master rejoicing, and you, shining waves of the lake, laugh with whatever of laughter is in store.

Poem 35

I would like you, piece of papyrus, to tell the tender poet/love poet, my comrade, Caecilius, to come to Verona, leaving behind the walls of Novum Comum and Lake Larius' shore: for I want him to receive certain thoughts of his friend and mine. Therefore, if he is wise, he will eat up the road although a thousand times his radiant girlfriend calls him back, going, and throwing both hands on his neck begs him to linger. She now, if true things are being announced to me, is desperately in love with him with a wild love: for from that time when she read the mistress of Dindymus having been begun, fires eat/have been eating the inner marrow of the unfortunate girl. I forgive you, girl more learned than the Sapphic muse: for the Great Mother has been begun attractively by Caecilius.

Poem 36

Annals of Volusius, defecated sheet of papyrus, fulfill a vow on behalf of my girlfriend. For she vowed to holy Venus and Cupid, that if I were restored to her and stopped brandishing savage iambs, she would give to the slow-footed god the "most choice" writings of the worst poet to be scorched by unlucky firewood, and the very bad girl understood that she was promising this to the gods playfully and wittily. Now, o one created from the blue sea, who cherishes holy Idalium and open Urii and Ancona and Cnidos full of reeds and Amathus and Dyrrachium, inn of the Adriatic, make/consider the vow received and paid back if it is not lacking in grace and unattractive. But meanwhile you come into the fire, annals of Volusius, full of the countryside and clumsiness, defecated sheet of papyrus.

Poem 40

What bad mind, tell me, wretched Raudus, drives you headlong into my iambs? What god not well summoned prepares to set in motion a mad fight for you? Or (is it) so that you may reach the mouth of the crowd? What do you want? Do you desire to be known no matter how? You will be, with a long punishment, since you wanted to love my beloved.

Poem 43

Hello, girl with a not very small nose and a not pretty foot and not black eyes and not long fingers and not dry mouth and not really very refined tongue. Girlfriend of the bankrupt (person) from Formiae, does the province say you are pretty? Is our/my Lesbia compared with you? O unwise and boorish generation!

Poem 44

O, estate of mine, whether Sabine or Tiburtine (for they say that you are Tiburtine to whom it is not pleasing to harm Catullus; but those to whom it is pleasing contend at any stake that you are Sabine), but whether Sabine or more truly Tiburtine, I was gladly in your country-house near the city, and I drove out a bad cough from my chest which my stomach gave me not undeserving while I was seeking extravagant dinners: for, while I wanted to be a Sestian guest, I read his speech, full of poison and pestilence, against the candidate, Antius. At this point a cold head cold and constant cough caused me to tremble violently, continually, until I fled into your breast, and cured myself with leisure and stinging nettle. In this way renewed I give you the greatest thanks because you did not avenge my mistake. Nor do I now pray to avert, if I take up the horrible writings of Sestius again, their coldness/flatness from bringing a head cold and cough, not to me, but to Sestius, himself, who invites me (only) at that time/then when I have read his bad book.

Poem 45

Septimius holding his love, Acme, on his lap says "My Acme, unless I love you to desperation and am not further prepared to love you continuously for all my years, as much as anyone is able to be perishing to the greatest extent, may I alone in Libya and parched India come face-to-face with a gray-eyed lion." When he said this, Love on the left as before on the right, sneezed approval.

But Acme gently bending back her head and having kissed with that glowing mouth of hers the drunk little eyes of her sweet boy says, "So my little Septimius, my life, may we continuously serve this one master just as a much greater and more fierce fire burns in my soft marrow." When she said this, Love on the left as before on the right, sneezed approval.

Now having set out from good auspices they love, are loved, with mutual enthusiasms. Unfortunate Septimius prefers his Amce alone to Syrias and Britains: faithful Acme finds her delight and instance of desire in Septimius alone. Who has seen any more fortunate people, who a love more auspicious?

Poem 46

Already spring is bringing back the unchilled warmth, already the fury of the equinoctial sky grows silent with the agreeable breezes of the west wind. Catullus, let the Phrygian fields be left behind and the rich territory of very hot Nicaea: let's fly to the famous cities of Asia. Now my mind, trembling in anticipation, is eager to wander, now my happy feet grow lively with eagerness. O sweet bands of comrades, farewell, whom, having set out far from home at the same time, various paths carry back in different ways .

Poem 49

Most skilled in speaking of the descendants of Romulus, as many as there are and as many as there have been, Marcus Tullius, and as many as there will be later in other years, Catullus, the worst poet of all, gives the greatest thanks to you, by so much the worst poet of all as you are the best advocate of all.

Poem 50

Yesterday, Licinius, at leisure we played a lot on my tablets, as it had been agreed that we would be self-indulgent: each of us writing light poetry played now in this meter, now in that, delivering mutually amid joking and wine. And I left there excited, Licinius, by your charm and wit, so that as a result food did not help poor me nor did sleep cover my little eyes with rest, but wild with madness I kept turning around on the whole bed, longing to see the daylight, so that I could talk with you and be with you at the same time. But after my limbs, tired with effort, lay half dead on the bed, I made this poem for you, delightful one, so that from it you might become aware of my pain. Now beware of being bold, and beware, I beg you, of spurning my prayers, darling, lest Nemesis demand punishment from you in return. She is a violent goddess; beware of hurting her/this one.

Poem 51

That man seems to me to be equal to a god, that man, if it is allowed, seems to surpass the gods, who sitting opposite again and again looks at and hears you sweetly laughing, which steals away all senses from poor me; for as soon as I have seen you, Lesbia, nothing of my voice remains for me in my mouth, but my tongue is numb, a thin flame runs down under my limbs, my ears ring with their own sound, my eyes are covered by twin night. Leisure, Catullus, is troublesome for you; you exult in your leisure and you act without restraint too much; leisure previously has destroyed both kings and fortunate cities.

Poem 60

It wasn't a lioness in the African mountains or Scylla barking from the lowest part of her groin that produced you with such a harsh and monstrous mind that you held despised the voice of a suppliant in his most recent misfortune, ah, one with too cruel a heart, was it?

Poem 64 (lines 50–253)

This bedspread, variegated with ancient images of people, shows the courage of heroes with amazing art. For gazing out at Dia's shore, resounding with the noise of waves, Ariadne bearing wild frenzies in her heart looks at Theseus withdrawing with his swift fleet, and not yet even does she believe she is looking at the things she is looking at, naturally since she then first roused from deceptive sleep, sees herself, unhappy, deserted on the lonely beach. But the forgetful young man, fleeing, strikes the shallow waters with his oars, abandoning his empty promises to the windy storm; from the seaweed far away the daughter of Minos with sad eyes like a stone statue of a Bacchant watches him, alas, watches and is in turmoil with great waves of cares, not keeping her delicate headdress on her golden head, not having clothed/not having been clothed with respect to her covered chest with her light cloak, not having bound/not having been bound with respect to her milk-white breasts with her smooth breastband, all of which things, having slipped here and there from her whole body, the waves of the sea played against before the feet of (the girl) herself. But then not caring about the lot of her headdress then of her flowing cloak she hung upon you, Theseus, from her whole heart, her whole feelings, her whole mind, lost. Ah unhappy one whom Venus drove crazy with constant mourning sowing thorny cares in her breast at that time when Theseus, bold in strength, having left the curved shores of Piraeus reached the Gortynian temples of the lawless king.

For they tell that at one time Athens, forced by a cruel plague to pay the penalty for Androgeos' slaughter, was accustomed to give choice young men and at the same time the glory of the unmarried women as a feast to the Minotaur. When the narrow walls were ravaged by these evils, Theseus himself chose to give up his own body on behalf of dear Athens rather than that such deaths in Athens, not deaths, be carried to Crete. And thus relying on his light ship and on gentle breezes he comes to bold Minos and his proud home. As soon as the royal young woman caught sight of this man with her longing eye, whom a pure bed breathing out pleasant odors was nourishing in the soft embrace of her mother, like (those of) the myrtles which the waters of the Eurotas produce or the different colors the spring breeze brings forth, not earlier did she turn away her blazing eyes from him than she conceived a flame from the bottom in her whole body and completely caught on fire in the bottom of her marrow. Alas, holy boy, wretchedly stirring up frenzies in your harsh heart, who mix the joys of people with cares, and you who rule Golgi and you who (rule) leafy Idalium, with what waves you have tossed the girl inflamed in her mind, often sighing for the golden guest! How great the fears she bore in her weak heart! How often then did she grow more pale than the radiance of gold when, desiring to contend against the savage monster, Theseus sought either death or the rewards of praise! Nevertheless, promising not unwelcome little gifts to the gods not in vain, she undertook her prayers with silent lip. For just as a wild whirlwind, twisting hard timber with its blast, uproots an oak shaking its arms on top of Mount Taurus or a conebearing pine with its sweating bark (far away it falls prone driven out by the roots, breaking over a large area all conceivable things in its way), so Theseus lay low the one savage in his subdued body tossing in vain his horns to the empty winds. From there, safe, with much praise he turned back his foot directing his wandering tracks with the thin thread so that the difficult-to-trace wandering about of the house would not delude him daparting from the labyrinthine curves.

But why should I, having digressed from the beginning of the poem, recall more things, how the daughter, leaving behind the face of her father, how the embrace of her sister, how finally of her mother, who (now) utterly lost used to delight in her poor daughter, chose the sweet love of Theseus over all these; or how, carried on a boat, she came to the foamy shores of Dia, or how her husband abandoned her bound with respect to her eyes in sleep leaving with his unmindful heart? They tell that she, raging in her burning heart, often poured forth clearsounding words from her deepest heart, and then sad ascended the very steep mountains, from where she could extend her eye onto the desolate tides of the sea, then ran forth into the hostile waves of the shaky sea lifting the soft coverings of her calf having been made bare, and sad had said these things in her last complaints, stirring up cold sobs from her wet mouth: "Thus, faithless (one), carried off from my native altars/home, faithless Theseus, did you abandon me on the deserted shore? Thus leaving with the power of the gods neglected, unmindful, ah, do you carry home your accursed false oaths? Could nothing bend the purpose of your cruel mind? Was there no clemency ready to you that your harsh heart might want to have compassion on me? But formerly you did not give these promises to me with your seductive words, not these did you ask me, unhappy, to hope for, but a happy marriage, but a desired wedding, all of which things, empty, the lofty winds are tearing to pieces. Now let no woman believe a man swearing, let no woman hope that the conversations of her husband are faithful, for whom, while their desiring mind is very eager to get something, they fear swearing nothing, they spare promising nothing; but as soon as the lust of their desiring mind has been satisfied, they remember their words not at all, they care about their false oaths not at all. Certainly I rescued you turning in the middle of a whirlwind of death, and I decided to lose my brother rather than fail you, deceptive, in your final danger. For this I will be given to wild beasts and birds as prey to be torn apart, and dead I will not be entombed with earth thrown on. Tell me, what lioness bore you under a lonely crag, what sea spit you out, conceived in the foaming waves, what Syrtis, what very greedy Scylla, what desolate Charybdis, (you) who give back such rewards for sweet life? If our marriage had not been dear to you, because you shuddered at the cruel rules of your ancient father, (yet) nevertheless you could have led me into your home to serve as a slave to you with agreeable labor, stroking your radiant feet with flowing water, or covering your bed with a purple bedspread. But why am I, driven out of my mind by evil, complaining in vain to the ignorant breezes, which, furnished with no senses cannot hear or give back words sent? He, moreover, is now turned almost in the middle of the waves, nor does anyone mortal appear on the empty seaweed. Thus, even cruel fortune mocking too much in my final danger has begrudged its ears to my complaints. Jupiter all powerful, would that at the first time the Athenian ships had not touched the Cretan shores, and the faithless sailor had not tied (up) his rope on Crete bringing terrible offerings to the unconquered bull, and that the evil guest hiding these cruel plans in his sweet beauty had not rested in my home! For where should I take myself? On what sort of hope, lost, do I depend? Should I seek the mountains of Ida? But the ferocious surface of the sea divides, separating with wide waters. Or should I hope for my father's help? The one whom I myself left having followed the young man sprinkled with my brother's slaughter? Or should I console myself with the faithful love of my husband? The one who is fleeing, bending his pliant oars in the waters? Moreover, the lonely island is cultivated by no house, an escape does not lie open because of the encircling waves of the sea. (There is) no method of flight, no hope of flight: all things are silent, all things are deserted, all things indicate death. Nevertheless my eyes will not grow weak with death nor will my senses leave from my tired body before I, having been betrayed, demand from the gods a just penalty and invoke the loyalty of the gods in my final hour. Therefore, Eumenides, punishing the deeds of men with avenging penalty, (you) whose foreheads surrounded with snaky hair carry in front the angers, breathing out, of your hearts, to here, to here draw near, listen to my complaints, which I, alas for unhappy me, poor, burning, blind with insane madness am forced to bring forth from the bottom of my marrow.

Since they are born true from the bottom of my heart, you, don't allow my mourning to vanish, but with the sort of mind Theseus left me alone, with such a mind, goddesses, let him make mournful himself and his own people."

After she poured forth these words from her sad breast, disturbed, demanding punishment for cruel deeds, the ruler of the gods nodded assent with his invincible divine power; with this movement the earth and rough seas trembled and the sky shook the flashing stars. Moreover, Theseus himself, beset with respect to his mind with a blind darkness, let go from his heart having forgotten all the instructions which earlier he held in his unchanging mind, and not raising on high the sweet signs for his sad father did not show that he was looking at the Athenian harbor safe and sound. For they tell that formerly, when Aegeus was entrusting his son to the winds for safekeeping, (his son) leaving the walls of the goddess with his fleet, having embraced him he gave instructions of such a kind to the young man: "One and only son more delightful to me by far than life, son, whom I am forced to let go into uncertain events, given back to me recently in the final end of old age, since my fortune and your burning courage snatch you away from me unwilling, whose weak eyes have not yet been sated with the dear image of my son, I, rejoicing with happy heart, will not let you go, nor will I allow you to carry signs of favorable fortune, but first I will bring out many complaints from my mind, making filthy my white hair with earth and dust poured on; then I will hang dyed sails on your wandering mast, so that the canvas darkened with Spanish rust may indicate my mourning and the fires (of love) of my mind. But if the inhabitant of holy Itonus, who nods assent to defend our race and the home of Erectheus, will have granted to you to sprinkle your right hand with the blood of the bull, then truly bring it about that these instructions flourish stored up in your mindful heart, that not any time cause them to be forgotten; that, as soon as your eyes will see our hills, the sails on all sides put down their mournful covering and that the twisted ropes raise on high radiant sails, so that seeing as soon as possible I may recognize joys in my happy mind, when a favorable time will establish you (as) returning." These instructions left Theseus holding them earlier in his unchanging mind, as clouds driven by a blast of the winds (leave) the lofty peak of a snowy mountain. But the father, as he was seeking a view from the top of the citadel, wearing out his disturbed eyes on constant weeping, as soon as he caught sight of the pieces of cloth of the puffed out sail, threw himself headlong from the top of the boulders, believing Theseus was lost to a bitter fate. Thus, having approached the dwelling of his home mournful because of his father's death, bold Theseus himself received such (mourning), the sort of mourning he had brought to Ariadne because of his unmindful mind. She then looking out, sad, at his ship leaving, wounded, turned over in her mind varied cares.

But on another part (of the bedspread) flourishing Bacchus was moving about rapidly with his cult group of Satyrs and with Sileni, born on Mount Nysa, seeking you, Ariadne, and inflamed by your love/love for you.

Poem 65

Although me, left lacking because of constant anguish, care calls away, Hortalus, from the learned maidens, and the mind (of my inclination) is not able to bring out the sweet offspring of the Muses, it is itself in turmoil because of such great misfortunes—for recently the flowing wave in the Lethean waters has wet the pale foot of my brother whom, snatched away from my eyes, the Trojan land crushes under the Rhoetean shore. . . . . Will I never see you hereafter, brother more worthy to be loved than life? But certainly I will always love (you), I will always sing songs sad because of your death, the sort that the Daulian one/Procne/the nightingale sings under the thick shades of the branches, lamenting the fate(s) of Itylus, removed by death.— But nevertheless, Hortalus, in such great mourning I send to you this translated poem of Callimachus, so that you do not think your words by chance flowed out of my mind entrusted in vain to wandering winds, as an apple of a betrothed husband sent as a secret gift runs forth from the pure lap of the maiden, (an apple) which, placed under soft clothing of the girl having forgotten, is shaken out while she leaps forward at the arrival of her mother, and it is driven headlong in its sloping fall, a conscious blush spreads on her sad face.

Poem 68 (lines 1–40)

That you, overwhelmed by chance and bitter misfortune, send me this short letter written on with tears, so that I might support a shipwrecked man thrown out by the foaming waves of the sea and restore him from the threshold of death, whom neither holy Venus allows to rest in soft sleep deserted in his unmarried bed, nor do the Muses delight with the sweet song of old writers, when his disturbed mind stays awake all night, that is pleasing to me, since you say that I am your friend and you seek from here gifts of the Muses and of Venus. But so that my afflictions are not unknown to you, Manlius, and so that you do not think I have an aversion to the duty of a guest/host, understand in what waves of fortune I myself am overwhelmed, so that you do not further seek happy gifts from unhappy me. At the time at which first the toga of a man was handed over to me, when my flourishing age was leading a delightful spring, I played around sufficiently much: the goddess is not unaware of me, (the goddess) who mixes sweet bitterness with cares. But all of this enthusiasm my brother's death has taken away from me because of mourning Oh, brother, taken away from unhappy me, you, you, brother, dying, have crushed my interests, my entire house has been overcome together with you; all of my joys have perished together with you which your sweet love nourished in life. Because of your untimely death I have driven away from my whole mind these enthusiasms and all delights of the mind. Therefore, as for the fact that you write that it is shameful for Catullus to be at Verona, because here whoever (is) of the better class warms his cold limbs in a deserted bed, it, Manlius, is not shameful, it is more nearly unhappy. You will forgive me if these duties, which mourning has taken away from me, I do not bestow on you when I cannot. For, the fact that there is not a great supply of literary work with me, this happens because I live at Rome: that is my home, that is my dwelling, there my time is consumed; (only) one of my many little book containers follows me here. Since this is so, I would not want you to decide that I am doing this because of an unkind mind or a not sufficiently generous inclination, that a supply of each thing has not been provided to you: I would confer it of my own accord, if there were any supply.

Poem 69

Do not wonder, Rufus, at why no woman wants to put her delicate thigh under you, not if you were to shake that one with the gift of loosely woven dress or the pleasure of a translucent stone. A certain nasty rumor harms you, in which a savage male goat is claimed to live under the valley of your armpits. All (the girls/women) fear this one, nor is it amazing: for the beast is powerfully nasty, nor would any charming girl lie down with him/it. Therefore, either kill the cruel plague of noses, or stop being surprised at why they flee.

Poem 70

My woman says that she prefers to marry no one more than me, not if Jupiter himself were to ask her. She says (this); but what a woman says to her eager lover, it is proper to write in wind and rapid water.

Poem 72

Once you used to say that you knew Catullus alone/that only Catullus knew you, Lesbia, and that you did not want to hold Jupiter before me. Then I esteemed you not only/not so much as the crowd (esteems) a girlfriend, but as a father esteems his sons/children and sons-in-law. Now I have gotten to know/know you; therefore, although I am on fire more excessively, nevertheless you are much more cheap and unimportant to me. How is this able (to be), you say? Because such an insult forces a lover to love more, but to like less.

Poem 76

If there is any pleasure to a person remembering earlier good deeds, when he thinks that he is devoted, and that he has not violated a sacred trust, and that he has not abused the divine power of the gods in any compact for the purpose of deceiving people, many joys remain in a long time, Catullus, prepared for you from this ungrateful love. For whatever things people are able to say or do well to anyone, these things have been said and done by you. All these things have perished, entrusted to an ungrateful mind. Therefore, why should you now torture yourself more? Why not make (yourself) firm in your mind and you, yourself, lead yourself back from there and stop being unhappy because/since/although the gods are unwilling? It is difficult to abandon suddenly a long love, it is difficult, but do this in any way it is pleasing; this is (your) one safety, this must be gained by you, do this, whether it is not able (to be done) or it is able. Oh gods, if it is characteristic of you to pity, or if ever you have brought final assistance to any people even then in death itself, look at unhappy me, and if I have led my life righteously, snatch away this plague and ruin from me which, creeping under me into the bottom of my limbs like a numbness, has driven out happiness from (my) whole heart. No longer do I look for that, that she esteem me in return, or what is not able (to be)/because she is not able, that she wish to be modest/chaste: I, myself, choose to be healthy and to abandon this foul disease. Oh gods, return this to me on behalf of my devotion.

Poem 77

Rufus, in vain and to no effect believed (to be) a friend to me (in vain? rather at great cost and misfortune), in this way did you creep under me and consuming my guts snatch away all good things, alas, from unhappy me? You snatched (them), alas, cruel poison of my/our life, alas, plague of our/my friendship.

Poem 84

"Hadvantages" Arrius used to say, if ever he wanted to say "advantages," and "hambush" (if ever he wanted to say) "ambush," and then he expected that he had spoken amazingly, whenever he said "hambush" to what degree/to the greatest degree he was able. I believe, so his mother, so his free maternal uncle, so his maternal grandfather had spoken and his grandmother. When he was sent into Syria everybody's ears had relaxed: they heard these same things (said) without aspiration and quietly, and afterwards they were not afraid for themselves of such words, when suddenly a terrifying message is/was brought, that the Ionian waves, after Arrius went there, now were not/no longer were Ionian, but "Hionian."

Poem 85

I hate and I love. Why I do this, perhaps you ask. I don't know, but I feel that it is happening and I am tortured.

Poem 86

Quintia is beautiful to many. To me she is radiant, tall, and straight (in posture): thus I admit these individual things, that whole "beautiful" I deny: for there is no charm, no grain of salt/wit in such a great body. Lesbia is beautiful, who not only is wholly aesthetically pleasing, but also alone has stolen all charms from all (people/women).

Poem 87

No woman is able to say truly that she was/has been loved to such an extent as you, my Lesbia, were/have been loved by me. No faith has ever been as great in any compact as was/has been found on my part in your love/my love for you.

Poem 96

If anything pleasing or welcome is able to happen for/is able to descend to/mute graves from our anguish, Calvus, through which longing we renew old loves and weep for friendships once let go, certainly untimely death for Quintilia is not for such great anguish as she rejoices in your love.

Poem 101

Having traveled through many peoples and many seas I come to these unhappy rites in honor of the dead, brother, so that I may present you with the final offering of death and may speak in vain to your silent ashes, since fortune has taken away you, yourself, from me, alas unhappy brother taken away undeservedly from me. Now meanwhile nevertheless, these things, which in the ancient custom of our parents/ancestors have been handed over as an unhappy offering for the rites of the dead, take, flowing much with brotherly tears, and forever, brother, hail and farewell.

Poem 109

You hold out a delightful thing to me, my life: that this love of ours between us is going to be permanent all the way. Great gods, bring it about that she is able to promise truly, and to say it faithfully and from (her) mind/desire/inclination, so that it may be permitted to us to lead/conduct, throughout (our) whole life, this eternal compact of holy friendship.

Poem 116

Often eagerly, with hunting mind, looking for how I could send you poems of Callimachus by which/ so that thereby I might placate you to me and so that you would not try to send hostile missiles all the way onto/continuously onto my head, now I see that this labor was taken on by me in vain, Gellius, and that my prayers from here/on these grounds have not prevailed. In return I will avoid those hurled missiles of yours (or) I will avoid those missiles of yours hurled against me, but pierced by mine, you will pay the penalty.

DISCUSSION QUESTIONS

The introductions to the poems in the Student Text (reprinted here) are intended not as summaries, but as jumping off points for thought and discussion. There I try to raise issues and possibilities rather than dictate conclusions. These introductions may be useful for beginning discussions in class. A general word of advice. Try to get the students to think in terms of how things *function* in the poems rather than what the poems are *about*. In this way you can avoid discussions that merely summarize content and can train students to engage in *analysis and argument*. What follows are the introductions to the poems from the Student Text along with some further ideas for discussion of the individual poems. Certainly the articles and books listed in the bibliography will provide you with many more ideas than I am able to include here.

Poem 1

Catullus' first poem is programmatic, that is, it "announces" what we are to expect from his poetry collection. But what is that "something" that we are led to expect? The enigmatic quality of this first poem avoids giving us an obvious answer or perhaps that is the answer. The poem leaves us with material to ponder: books, gifts, charm, newness, literary undertakings, giving, polishing, literary support, patron/client, size, number, virginity, attractiveness, questions/answers, time, history, Italy, self/other, modesty, pride, divinity, learning, work. Its seeming simplicity—a two-line question, a five-line answer, a three-line conclusion—teases us with a multivalent program. It is an offering/gift to Cornelius, but heralds a readership and posterity beyond his specificity.

- Discuss how Catullus characterizes his work in this poem. What specific words does he use about his work? How does this characterization fit with the concerns of the neoteric poets?
- What is the relationship between Catullus and Cornelius Nepos as it is revealed in the poem?
  Who was Nepos?
  Does that matter in terms of Catullus' choice of him for addressee?
  Several lines focus on the work of Nepos. To what effect?
- Discuss the issue of "time" in the poem. Pick out each word that has temporal significance.
- How does "divinity" appear in the poem?
- What "number" words appear in the poem? Compare the importance of numbers and counting in Poems 5 and 7.
- Compare the discussion of "books" in Poem 22, where the word "pumice" reappears.
- Discuss the nature of gift giving in the poem. What is being given to whom? What are three other poems of Catullus that are concerned with "gifts"?

Poem 2

*Longing, desire, and their relief—provocative behavior and play—participation and separation—initiation and response—possession—of a bird—of a girl—lack of fulfillment—these are several of the issues at stake in this poem. A dizzying eight lines, introduced by the word "**passer**," is followed by two simpler final lines, which through their first word, "**tecum**," reveal the **passer** of the first line to be both the poem's addressee and an object of the speaker's desire.*

- Discuss who has desire for what or for whom in the poem. What is the Latin evidence for this? Compare the dynamics of the "participants" in this poem with those found in Poem 51.

- The possessive word "meae" in line 1, suggests an intimacy between the speaker and his "puella." How does the rest of the poem support or not support this notion?

- "Active" and "passive" sexual roles had different value to the Romans. What role does the "puella" play here? How does that connect with larger Roman social and cultural values?

- In which other poems by Catullus is the idea of "play" important?

Poem 3

*This dirge for a pet sparrow is mournful, tender, and funny. Its melodramatic mock-elegiac tone is offset by strongly affectionate language. To see the poem as solely romantic or solely comic is to miss the careful way in which it manages to be both. The subject of the **passer** of course recalls Poem 2.*

- How does the "passer" line Poems 2 and 3?

- What is the effect of the repetition of "meae puellae," each time in the same metrical position, in lines 3,4,17? How does this recall Poem 2?

- How is "affection" embedded in this poem?

- Compare the partially solemn tone of this poem with the tone of Poem 101. What elements in this poem open the door to levity, a feature certainly not present in Poem 101.

Poem 4

In this poem Catullus evokes the "life" and "retirement" of a little ship by playing off funerary and dedicatory literary genres. Through extensive PERSONIFICATION, the boat "flies and speaks," beams of wood "swim," oars are "little palms," foliage is "hair," the ship "ages." The poem's meter, pure iambic trimeter, is effective for creating a sense of speed. The language of the poem is highly elaborate, with epic diction, LITOTES, and repeated alternatives (whether...or). While many would like to connect this poem with Catullus' return from Bithynia following military service, there is nothing in the poem, itself, that necessitates this. Poems 10, 31, and 46, often seen in this same context, unlike this poem, all specify place and speaker. Thomson and Glasgow (cf. Thomson's Catullus *[1997] pp. 213–214) raise the interesting possibility that this poem may be a translation or adaptation by Catullus of a lost "Phaselus of Berenice" (cf. vocabulary, line 1) by Callimachus along the lines of Poem 66, Catullus' translation of Callimachus' "Lock of Berenice." Berenice II was queen of Egypt in the 3rd century BCE and Callimachus wrote a number of poems in her honor.*

- List all of the ways in which the "phaselus" is personified in the poem.
- What makes the language of the poem "learned"?
- Follow the route of the "phaselus" on the map on page 14 of the Student Text.
- How is "speech" a central issue in the poem?

Poem 5

Living/dying, human time/nature's time, calculating/losing track, knowing/not knowing, light/night, kisses and more kisses. Central to this poem is the notion of what has value. (Recall this same issue from Poem 1 where Nepos' valuing of Catullus' "worthless stuff" makes him worthy of being a dedicatee.) Here, the strict moral code of the gossiping old men is to be "counted" as worthless, while the kisses of the oppositional life of making love are to be "counted" repeatedly (and then confused). It is interesting that the "oppositional" life incorporates the language of what it claims to oppose. Must the erotic be quantified?

- What associations does Catullus' use of the pseudonym "Lesbia" give to his poetry?
- How do "counting" and "valuing" feature in this poem? Compare Poem 1 for the importance of Nepos' valuing of Catullus' work. Who is doing the "valuing" here? What would the "rather strict old men" value, perhaps, that Catullus does not?
- In what way do the "quis malus" and the "old men" function similarly?
- Compare the role of "outsiders" in this poem and in Poem 2.
- The build-up of numbers in this poem is extraordinary. What is its effect?
- How does Catullus use the images of "night" and "light" in this poem?

Poem 7

While the centrality of kissing directly connects this poem with Poem 5, its learned language and form of question and reply produce a very different, more cerebral, effect. Yet the seemingly cerebral response, in turn, contains "hot" sand and voyeuristic (?) stars. The intellectual control of the speaker is called into question by his characterization of himself as "crazy" and the comfort of his answer is threatened by the feared intrusion of others who would deny him his pleasure.

- Compare Poem 7 with Poem 5. The "kissing" connection is obvious. What makes them very different poems? Are numbers and counting treated in the same way? What is the effect of the word "basiationes" (line 1) vs. "basia" (line 9)?
- In what way are "outsiders" present in this poem?
- What is the effect of the speaker's shift from the first person "mihi" (line 1) to the third person "Catullo" (line 10)?
- Why does the speaker use the word "vesano" (line 10)? What does "craziness" have to do with kissing?
- Who was Callimachus? Why does that matter for understanding this poem?
- What is "Callimachean" or "Hellenistic" about the way Callimachus is referred to in this poem?

Poem 8

The speaker begins and ends by telling himself to persist in detaching himself from his love affair, but along the way offers dreamy recollection, uncontrolled anger and jealousy, and emotional swings. The obsessive questions to the girl in the future tense are a counterpoint to the almost hypnotic evocation of the past.

- Compare "desinas ineptire" with "inepte" in Poem 12, line 4. What is the "inappropriateness" of each behavior described?
- What is the effect of the switching of "persons" in the poem? Who occupies the spot of "second person"? Who of "third"? Are these static positions?
- Catullus addresses himself as "miser" in this poem. Where else in the poems is the adjective "miser" used and what is its emotional effect?
- Discuss "pacing" in this poem. When does the language seem to move slowly and when does it seem to speed up? Why?
- Compare the notion of "saying goodbye" to a beloved in this poem with that found in Poem 11.
- Compare the tone of Poem 76 to that of this poem. What makes them different?

Poem 10

Central to this poem is a humorous portrayal of social anxiety. After depicting himself as part of the military that got "screwed over" by a shameless governor, the speaker in turn feels "screwed over" when Varus' lover questions his financial success and forces him to lie to cover up his inadequacy. He retaliates by removing her from "membership in his club" of "charming" people. (The narrative structure, the colloquial tone, the dialogue, the social anxiety, the wit are all elements seen later in Horace's Satire 1.9.) The notion of what is charming and attractive operates for Catullus simultaneously on the erotic, aesthetic, and social levels.

- Compare the function of "otium" in this poem with that in Poems 50 and 51.
- Is the "scortillum" charming or not? Why does the speaker use insulting language about her in line 24?
- In what way are "power," "status," and "wealth" important to this poem?
- Compare the colloquial tone and language of this poem with that found in Horace <u>Satire</u> 1.9.
- Explain how "cinaediorem" (line 24) and "irrumator" (line 12) relate to sexual/social power and, more generally, to Roman values.

Poem 11

Poems 11 and 51 are linked in the Catullan corpus by their Sapphic meter (which only appears in these two poems) and their recollection of Sappho's poetry. (See Poem 51 for more extensive comments on Catullus' use of Sappho.) Poem 11 can be seen to fall into two seemingly disparate yet closely entwined parts, lines 1–16 and lines 17–24. The wide-ranging political/military landscape of the first part of the poem—land to be potentially crossed/assaulted by the speaker and his male comrades—is narrowed, in the second part, to the farthest part of a meadow where love has fallen like a flower grazed by the aggressive/female/castrating plough. The "male bonding" of Catullus and his comrades is replaced by that of three hundred male lovers and the feminized land to be conquered is turned into the fragile flower/love belonging to a man. How are gender, power, and love situated in the poem? Is writing brilliantly about one's castration a sign of victory or defeat?

- Discuss how the "masculine" and the "feminine" function in this poem.
- Discuss the image of the flower.
- How does the imagined military travel of the poem's beginning fit with the poem's conclusion?
- Discuss "space" and "position" as well as "active" and "passive" in the poem.
- Discuss the Sapphic connection between this poem and Poem 51.
- Discuss the interest in "numbers" in the poem. Which other poems show a similar interest?

Poem 12

Through an attack on the poor manners of a napkin "thief," this poem articulates what isn't considered funny at a dinner party of Catullus' set. The light humor which begins the poem segues into an affectionate tribute to Catullus' friends, Fabullus and Veranius, who sent the napkin to him as a gift while away serving in Spain. Presence, absence, sending, stealing—these dichotomies hover over this "article of remembrance" which functions as substitute "object of love."

- Discuss how this poem, like Poems 1 and 5, shows interest in the issue of "value."
- What is the role of friendship in this poem?
- Which other poems in this text are concerned with gifts, memory, and wit?
- What role does Pollio play in the poem?
- What possible function for poetry emerges from lines 10–11?

Poem 13

A charming, "anti-invitation" poem that celebrates friendship and love through delicate play on the guest/host relationship. Fabullus must bring almost everything, despite his status as guest, while the "impoverished" host, who seems to have nothing, will make a gift of a gift that will more than meet his guest's desires. Fullness/emptiness, guest/host, giving/receiving, human/divine all blend in an elegant and humorous social romp.

- What are the conditions imposed on Fabullus' dining well?
- Discuss the ambiguity of what the host has to offer.
- Discuss the elements of "surprise" in the poem.
- How does the "puella" function in this poem?

Poem 14a

In the context of warm teasing about a gift of bad poetry he has received from his friend, Calvus, Catullus plays again with ideas about gifts, aesthetic sensibilities, patrons and clients, teasing, wit, and exchange. Compare Poem 1 where Catullus presents his own book as well as Poem 13 with its surprise gift. In this poem, Calvus' gift giving calls for gift giving in response.

This poem evokes the world of the comraderie of the neoteric poets at Rome.

- Discuss poetry's role as a "weapon" in this poem. Compare Poem 12, lines 10-11.
- On Calvus, compare Poems 50 and 96 (in the Student Text), as well as Poem 53 (not contained there).
- How would you characterize the friendship between Calvus and Catullus in this poem?

Poem 22

What one is like as a person and what one is like as a writer may not match. The personal stylishness of Suffenus does not carry over to his poems. Though the "package" is polished, the substance is not. Suffenus' self-delusion is declared to be part of the self-delusion in which all human beings engage in some regard. This poem may be compared with Poem 1 for issues of poetic production and value.

- Discuss all the Latin terms in this poem that relate to the materiality of writing.
- How does the use of the word "pumice" in this poem compare with that in Poem 1, line 2?
- Teachers who want to follow up on the issue of the alleged distinction between "poet" and "poetry" may want to read Poem 16 (not in the Student Text). Because of the especially graphic sexual vocabulary in that poem, it is not likely to end up on the AP* syllabus. However, it is a very important poem in the Catullan corpus.
- Does the general comment about self-deception at the end of the poem affect one's perception of or attitude towards Suffenus? Why or why not?

Poem 30

This poem, addressed to a man, deals with love and trust. These issues are treated again in very similar fashion in Poem 76, addressed to a woman. Forgetting and remembering, the gods, deception and trustworthiness, words and deeds, all appear in both poems. Cf. Poem 70, line 4, for the idea of a lover's speech that should be written in wind and water. Seeing these issues in the context of a male lover and beloved should remind the reader that Catullus wrote poems about men desiring men as well as men desiring women. The meter is used only here in the poems of Catullus.

- Discuss the vocabulary of trust and betrayal in the poem.
- Discuss past, present, and future in the poem.
- How does "memory" function in the poem?
- Compare this poem with Poem 76.

Poem 31

A joyful return home after military service abroad in Bithynia is the occasion for this poem. The happy sight of home and its attendant rest and pleasure are the only balance for the overseas burdens of the returning soldier. The PERSONIFICATION of Sirmio enhances the sense that "place" has the power to move the speaker profoundly.

- Discuss the language of pleasure and comfort in the poem.
- Compare this poem with Poem 46. How are travel and home characterized in each?
- What are some of the stylistic features that lend a studied elegance to the poem?

---

* AP is a registered trademark of the College Entrance Examination Board, which was not involved in the production of, and does not endorse, this product.

Poem 35

Reading, writing, love, friendship, worship, and travel all come together in this poem of literary and erotic journeys—begun and delayed. The triangle (quadrangle? pentagon?) of the speaker, Caecilius, the girl, the unspecified mutual friend (?), and the papyrus (?), is the image within which this poem of request and of forgiveness for its possible lack of fulfillment takes shape. The "thoughts" that the speaker wants Caecilius to receive are never identified and they give way to a sympathetic and gently humorous understanding on the speaker's part of the power of his friend Caecilius' words. Perhaps the possible literary advice for completion to be offered in Verona yields to mutual admiration by the speaker and the girl for the intellectual and erotic power of the poem begun.

- Discuss how poetry and passion are intertwined in this poem.
- How does Caecilius' girlfriend function in the poem? How is she characterized?
- Where else does Sappho appear in the poems of Catullus contained in the Student Text? What similarities are there between the girl in Poem 35 and the speaker in Poem 51?

Teachers interested in further material on the worship of Cybele should read Poem 63.

Poem 36

In this poem the speaker playfully "reinterprets" the vow of his girlfriend in order to delicately tease her and win her back. The method is the substitution (and simultaneous trashing) of the writings of Volusius for his own wicked verses. The deity who is to receive the literary burnt offering is, appropriately, Venus, the goddess of love.

- What one "says" versus what one "means" is an important issue in the Catullan corpus.
- Discuss how the speaker "reinterprets" his girlfriend's words and to what effect.
- Compare the tricky interpretations of the superlatives in line 6 ("electissima" and "pessimi") with the play on "worst" and "best" in Poem 49.
- Locate on a map all of the places of Venus' worship mentioned in the poem.

Poem 40

In this poem the speaker counters the perceived offense done to him by a man who wanted to love his beloved with his own power to attack that man with words. The poem builds up suspense by leaving until the last line the explanation of the offense (you wanted to love...). Compare Poem 11 where the image of the speaker's castrated love is in some sense countered by his ability to memorialize his castrator, Lesbia, in words.

- Compare Poem 14a for poetry as a "weapon."
- Discuss how poetry becomes imbedded in sexual power play.
- Compare the surprise ending here with that in Poem 13.

Poem 43

While enumerating the defects of the girlfriend of Mamurra, the speaker simultaneously sets up an ideal of female attractiveness, condemns both Mamurra and his girlfriend, and indirectly compliments Lesbia, his own girlfriend.

- Pick out the specific Latin words in this poem that are connected with beauty (or lack of beauty).
- Which other poems in the Student Text address the issue of "taste" found in the poem's last line? (Compare, for example, Poems 12 and 50.)
- What is the effect of the move to a general statement in the poem's final line?
- Examine the structure of the poem. It has two units of four lines. How does the anaphora of "nec" reinforce this structure? Line 5 is an extended vocative phrase. How does this give the addressee prominence? What is the effect of not naming her, considering the naming of Lesbia in line 7? What is the effect of the two rhetorical questions and the final exclamation?

Poem 44

A compliment to the curative powers of his country home involves a humorous attack on the bad writings of Sestius, who requires his dinner guests to read his writing as a condition for their invitation. Reading such "cold" writing as Sestius' induces a "cold" in the speaker, who would prefer to shift the ill effect of the reading onto the writer.

- Compare the "effects" of writing here (reading bad writing makes you "sick") and in Poem 22, where Suffenus seems to be someone different when he writes.
- Discuss the social context of the poem—country home, dinner invitations, sharing of writing etc.

Poem 45

The exquisite balance of these extravagant declarations of love contains competitive amatory rhetoric. The statement of mutual love leads to two questions about the lovers and their love: who has seen more fortunate people, who a more auspicious love? Much of how one interprets the poem hinges on whether one takes these as rhetorical questions or not. Do they confirm the uniqueness of this love or do they, by utilizing comparative language, extend the "intramural" competition between the lovers to an "extramural" game of love?

- Compare this poem with Horace *Odes* 3.9 (useful for those teaching AP* Horace and AP* Catullus as well as for those teaching a Catullus/Horace Latin Lyric class at the college level).
- Discuss how balance and competition work in the poem.
- Ask the students whether they would like to be one half of this couple. Why? Why not?
- What is the effect of ending the poem with (rhetorical) questions?

---

* AP is a registered trademark of the College Entrance Examination Board, which was not involved in the production of, and does not endorse, this product.

Poem 46

There is a joyous momentum to this poem which includes an almost wistful recognition of the abandonment of a common purpose. Eager departure from the land of military service occasions saying farewell to sweet friends. The almost complete absence of ELISION *in the poem and the repetition of the word* **iam** *at the beginning of lines 1 and 2, and then at the beginning of lines 7 and 8, creates an almost staccato marching effect.*

- Compare this poem with Poem 31.
- How is spring characterized in the poem?
- Discuss carefully the vocabulary of lines 10-11 in terms of how it evokes distance, travel, movement etc.

Poem 49

Seven lines of great simplicity and complexity link Catullus with the famous Marcus Tullius Cicero. The elaborate use of ANAPHORA, *superlatives, repetition of phrases, and formal language show Catullus carefully crafting a poem out of few and fairly simple words. The poem adopts a tone of self-deprecation and homage to a great speaker, but that may belie an* IRONIC *subtext.*

- Discuss the social/historical context of the poem. Identify Cicero. If the students are reading Cicero's *Pro Caelio* as the other part of the AP* Latin Literature curriculum, use this opportunity to introduce that speech.
- Note the use of devices like anaphora which are common to Cicero's oratorical prose.
- Discuss the potential for irony in the poem.
- Compare the use of superlatives in this poem with that in Poem 36.

Poem 50

Leisure, writing, pleasure, and desire are all intertwined in this poem. Memories of "play" between Catullus and his intimate friend, Calvus, lead to future desires. The idea of **otium** *or "leisure" and what it allows time for in this poem should be recalled when reading Poem 51, which follows.*

- Find all the uses of the word "otium" or related words in Catullus' poems or in the poems of Catullus in the Student Text. Compare the idea of "otium" in Poems 10 and 51.
- What evidence can one use to find an erotic level in this poem?
- Discuss the temporal sequence in the poem.
- Where else does Calvus appear in the Catullan corpus or in the Catullus poems in the Student Text?

---

* AP is a registered trademark of the College Entrance Examination Board, which was not involved in the production of, and does not endorse, this product.

Poem 51

This poem is a translation/adaptation/interpretation of Sappho Poem 31. (It is linked to Poem 11 by its Sapphic meter, which only appears in these two poems, as well as its recollection of Sappho.) Cf. the English translation of Sappho Poem 31 included here. Some of the similarities between Sappho's poem and Catullus' poem will be apparent: both deal with the effects of desire, issues of the self, and a third figure beyond speaker and object of desire. There are several significant changes Catullus has made from his "original," including the fact that his speaker is male, not female, and his addressee is named. We are dealing here with heterosexual not homoerotic desire and the object of that desire has a name, "Lesbia." The specificity of "naming," though, is countered by the multivalence of the particular name, for "Lesbia" (as P. Allen Miller has captured it [cf. Lyric Texts and Lyric Consciousness *pp. 101ff.]) is in fact a "triple-faceted" object of desire. For who is Lesbia? She is poetic construct/pseudonym, Clodia, and Sappho (the famous poet from Lesbos) herself. This poem is about passionate engagement—with a woman, with a poet, with one's own literary/erotic self.*

Sappho, Poem 31 (English translation from the Greek)

That man seems to me to be equal to the gods, who sits opposite you and nearby hears you sweetly speaking and charmingly laughing, a thing which truly excites my heart in my breast; for whenever I see you for a moment, then for me to say anything is no longer possible, but my tongue is broken in silence and immediately a thin flame has stolen under my skin, and I see nothing with my eyes, and my ears make a buzzing sound, and cold sweat possesses me, and trembling seizes me completely, and I am greener than grass, and I seem to myself to be lacking little to be dead. But everything must be ventured, since...even a needy person...

- Compare the idea of "otium" in Poems 10 and 50.
  Compare this poem with Sappho, Poem 31.
- Compare this poem with Poem 11, the only other poem in the Catullan corpus written in the same meter.
- Read and discuss some of the scholarship that compares the two poems. (See the Bibliography in this book.)
- Discuss how desire is evoked in the poem.

Poem 60

This poem is one long sentence, a five-line outraged question. Its power comes from the wildness of its language and imagery and the lack of specificity given to a particular situation. What emerges is a carefully constructed emotional outburst that utilizes material as old as Homer's Odyssey *(cf. Book 12. 86–100 on Scylla). For Scylla and the word* leaena, *see Ariadne's impassioned questions to Theseus in Poem 64, lines 154–57. Dido, in Vergil's* Aeneid *Book 4. 366–67, uses the same idea of "wild animal parentage" to express her belief in Aeneas' hardheartedness.*

- Read the passage in Homer noted above (in Greek or in English translation) and discuss its connection with this poem.
- Read the Vergil material noted above (in Latin or in English translation) and discuss its relevance to the poem.
- Compare this poem with the lines from Poem 64 noted above.
- Discuss how Catullus creates a sense of outrage in the poem.

Poem 64 (lines 50–253)

Poem 64, by far Catullus' longest, at over 400 lines, belongs to the genre called in modern times the "epyllion" or mini-epic. Written in dactylic hexameter, the meter of epic, an epyllion deals with epic material but in a smaller and different way. It often gives a new focus to familiar material, shows interest in description and psychological matters, and uses allusions for identification rather than obvious names. Poem 64 is the only surviving example of the genre in Latin, although there is evidence of others, including the Io *of Calvus and the* Zmyrna *of Cinna (cf. Poem 95, which is not in this text). Poem 64 is an account of the wedding of the mortal, Peleus, and the goddess, Thetis, who produce the child, Achilles. Lines 50–253 of the poem, the selection given in this text, is the story of Ariadne and Theseus and her abandonment by him, which is depicted on the bedspread of Peleus and Thetis. Some would argue that Catullus' Poem 64 is heavily influenced by Callimachus, who wrote a similar "ec-phrastic" epyllion, that is, one including a literary description of an object. It should be noted that this "story within a story" is longer than its "frame." The happy theme of marriage has contained within it the sobering tale of an unhappy love. Whether heavily influenced by Callimachus or not, Poem 64—and the specific selection here—recalls at the level of theme and language much that is found elsewhere in Catullus' poems. The themes of love, abandonment, memory/forgetting, death, vengeance, family, divinity, the male hero/imperialist, gifts or offerings, all have echoes throughout the collection.*

- Read all of Poem 64 (in English translation, since it is long, or selected passages in Latin)
- and discuss how the passage in the Student Text fits into the poem as a whole. Use this as an opportunity to discuss the Greek figures, Peleus, Thetis, Theseus, Ariadne, the Minotaur etc.
- Discuss the thematic issues that are common to this selection of Poem 64 (love, abandonment etc.), as well as other poems of Catullus.
- Discuss love and gender identification. What sort of "hero" is Theseus here? What sort of "hero" is Ariadne? What happens when epic, erotic, and familial values converge?
- Note the lines that have a spondaic fifth foot (see the notes in the Student Text) and discuss the effect (if any) of that slowing down of the line.
- Discuss what makes Poem 64 a "little epic" (consider meter, theme, narrative etc.).

Poem 65

Poem 65, like Poems 68 and 101, refers to the death of Catullus' brother. Here, grief is seen as a barrier to Catullus' production of poetry—or is it? Carefully embedded in this poem of lament is another tale of love and sadness (the final SIMILE*) through which Catullus confirms that even sorrow does not make him forget his friend's literary request. This poem serves as an elaborate introduction to Poem 66, the translation of a Callimachus poem that follows in the text of Catullus.*

- Discuss the various poems that mention the death of Catullus' brother. How are they similar or different?
- Which other poems in the Catullan corpus or in the Student Text address the issue of the circumstances of poetic production? Discuss how this makes "art" and "life" interactive.
- Discuss other poems where grief or pain of some kind leads to writing/words (cf. Ariadne in Poem 64, Poem 50, and Poem 101).

Poem 68 (lines 1–40)

Scholars have debated whether Poem 68, lines 1–40, is a complete poem by itself or is connected with the lines that follow. More see the two as distinct. Since only lines 1–40 are included here, comments will be limited to that material alone. A request for "gifts of the Muses and of Venus" opens up into an emotional world that links brotherly love and loss to the ability to supply others with gifts of love and writing. Compare the very different handling of brotherly loss in this poem from that in Poem 101, despite the phrase that is identical in both poems. In Poem 101 there is a "separation" of brotherly loss from all else. Here it reverberates with the rest of the speaker's life.

- Compare this selection from Poem 68 with Poem 101.
- How is "brotherly" love related to "other" love in this poem?
- Discuss the connection between love and writing in the poem.
- Read all of Poem 68 (in English or selected parts in Latin) and discuss how this selection fits with the whole poem.

Poem 69

This poem makes an allegation about smelly armpits in a humorous and kind of sexy way. Its "charming" description of the "uncharming" recalls the similar interplay in Poem 10. The HYPERBOLE *of the beastly image of disgusting smell plays off the enticing images of the women to clever effect. Notice how the* **trux...caper** *hides in the middle of the poem in the "valley" between the women!*

- Compare the issue of writing charmingly about uncharming things in this poem and Poem 10.
- How does Catullus make disgusting material funny and sexy?

Poem 70

This poem circles around the (un)reliability of speech and the power(lessness) of writing. What appears at first glance to be two lines of positive declaration followed by two lines of scepticism is more layered than that, for the first couplet is not about what "is" but about what "is said," while the second couplet further complicates matters by the introduction of "writing."

- Discuss how speech, writing, and love are intertwined in the poem. Which, if any, are trustworthy or enduring?
- Discuss how reading line 2 makes one rethink line 1.
- What is the effect of Jupiter's appearance in the poem? (Remember Jupiter is married and has affairs.) Compare the function of Jupiter in Poem 72 and Poem 7.
- Which other poems in the Catullan corpus or in the Student Text combine love and divinity?

Poem 72

Different kinds of love and the connection (or disconnect) between knowing and loving are at the heart of this poem. Where does valuing fit or not fit with loving?

- Compare Jupiter in this poem and Poems 7 and 72.
- Discuss the importance of comparative words in the poem.
- What are the ambiguities in the first two lines?
- Place the poem in its social/historical context by discussing the relationship a father had with his sons and sons-in-law. What is the effect of the introduction of that relationship into the context of love for a girlfriend? What is the role of the "vulgus" in the poem?

Poem 76

The solemn and religious tone to this self-appeal contrasts with Poem 8's tension between reason and emotion. Both deal with abandoning a love, but the effect is quite different. The appeal to the gods and the declaration by the speaker of his sense of devotion put love and its consequences in a larger Roman social and cultural context.

- Compare this poem with Poem 8 and Poem 30. Discuss what effect (if any) the gender of the love object (female in 8 and 76, male in 30) has on the poem.
- Discuss the notion of a "foedus" in this poem and in Poems 87 and 109.
- Discuss the characterization of love as a "disease." Compare the effect of love in this poem with that in Poem 51.
- Compare the notion of love as "torture" here (line 10) and in Poem 85.

Poem 77

The tortured feeling of this poem concerning friendship betrayed comes in part from its lengthy postponement of its first main verb until the poem's third line. The poem has just three main verbs, one of which is just a repeat of or answer to another. The elaborate frame of vocatives in the poem makes it a kind of crying out in disbelief, rage, and sorrow.

- Discuss the identity of Rufus.
- Compare the notion of betrayal in this poem with that in Poem 76.
- How many vocatives are there in the poem? What is their cumulative effect?

Poem 84

The unsophisticated Arrius doesn't know when to start a Latin word with an h. *Trying to imitate the educated, he puts the letter in where it doesn't belong. He becomes the butt of a joke about social circumstances and language. At the time Catullus was writing, the issue of aspiration (production of the breathy* h *sound) was being written about (Caesar had a section on it in his* On Analogy*) and linguistic practice was not consistent. Arrius' pronunciation may arise from his rustic dialect or from excessive (and incorrect) imitation of urban, more educated, speakers of Latin.*

- Discuss the social implications of "correct" speech.
- Discuss the presence or absence of "h" in the Romance Languages.
- Discuss elision as an area in which the "weakness" of "h" is apparent.

Poem 85

In this cryptic, consummate, love poem who is there besides an "I'? The only "you" is that in **requīris**. *And who is that? Has the relationship of reader to speaker preempted that of speaker to lover? Or are the two somehow elided? Notice the progression in the poem from active to passive verbs, with the ambiguous* **fĩerī** *at the "crossroads."*

- Discuss how such a short poem (two lines) can do so much. Look at structure, word order, vocabulary, voice and person of verbs, meter, etc.
- Compare the issue of love as "torture" here and in Poem 76, line 10. Since "crucifixion" was used as a method of punishing slaves, what are some of the class and power issues evoked by the vocabulary of this poem?
- Discuss the "you" of the poem.

Poem 86

Is the whole merely the sum of its parts? Obviously not. Without the "Venus-like quality" of "sex appeal" there is no real attractiveness. The idea that Lesbia becomes attractive through an act of "theft" (the same verb is used of "stealing" kisses in the first and last words of Poem 99) puts a spicy twist on the notion of the possession of, or the acquiring of, sexual appeal.

- Compare this poem with Poem 43. In each case, how is Lesbia portrayed as "different"?
- How does the speaker separate himself from "the many" in this poem?
- *Is* a woman "formosa" or is she *perceived* as such?
- Discuss the notion that Lesbia's "sex appeal" involves "theft."

Poem 87

There are echoes here of Poem 8 and its declaration that Lesbia has been loved as no other has been loved. But rather than the extreme mood swings of that poem, here there is a self-satisfaction in the speaker's sense of his having loved in a certain manner despite anything else.

- Compare this poem with Poem 8. How does the tone differ?
- What is the effect of the anaphora of "nulla" and the use of the correlatives "tantum...quantum" and "tanta...quanta"?

Poem 96

This one sentence, six lines long, is Catullus' poem of consolation on the occasion of the death of Quintilia, Calvus' wife or girlfriend. We know from Propertius (Elegies 2.34.89–90) that Calvus wrote an elegy on the death of Quintilia. From a fragment of Calvus' writings, forsitan hoc etiam gaudeat ipsa cinis *(fr.16 Morel in* Fragmenta Poetarum Latinorum epicorum et lyricorum praeter Ennium et Lucilium *[1927], ed. W. Morel), likely from that elegy, we can imagine that Catullus' poem (cf.* certe...gaudet) *takes off from what Calvus has already written. The lack of specificity, starting with the word* **nostrō,** *about the identity and number of the individuals ex-periencing* **dolor, dēsīderium, amor,** *and* **amīcitia** *makes this poem more enigmatic than it may appear to be.*

- Discuss how the intricacy and lack of specificity in this poem makes this "consolation" poem rather complicated.
- Compare this poem with others that involve Calvus.
- Compare this poem with Poem 101 in terms of what the dead can know or feel.

Poem 101

The somber and isolated dignity of this poem about Catullus' brother's death is perhaps unparalleled in his poems. The contrast between the "mute ashes" of the brother who has died and the perpetual voice of the poet saying "hail and farewell" entails a complicated commentary on the concept of loss.

- Discuss the purpose of mourning the dead. For whom do Catullus' words have meaning?
- Compare the selection from Poem 68 in terms of how it treats the brother's death.
- Discuss how the poem can function for the speaker, for the dead, for the larger audience.

Poem 109

What in its first line may appear to be a simple proposal for lovemaking opens up into fervent prayer to the gods that they bring it about that the speaker's lover speaks and promises truly. The almost solemn elegance of the poem's last line—with its language of sacred accord—is predicated precariously upon the speaker's wish that his lover's voice is to be trusted.

- The synchysis, or interlocked word order, reflects perhaps the lovers union. Discuss how the speaker's hopes for girlfriend to be "promising truly" and "speaking sincerely" call into question the stability that the figure of synchysis might suggest.
- The word "vita" is used in both lines 1 and 5. How does its reappearance in a somewhat different sense in line 5 affect its interpretation in line 1?

Poem 116

This is one of a group of hostile poems addressed to Gellius which, in turn, form part of a larger group of Catullan poems of aggressive attack. Here a present of poetry is mentioned as having been a possible vehicle for calming hostilities, but, due to the failure of that, the fight continues. This is the last poem in the Catullan corpus.

- Discuss the metrically noteworthy aspects of this poem.
- Compare Poem 7 and Poem 65 for references to Callimachus.
- Discuss how the poems of Callimachus function in the "war" between the speaker and Gellius.

Sample Test Questions

I strongly recommend that teachers of Advanced Placement* courses obtain from the College Board its publication containing previous AP* Latin exams. Students will benefit greatly from practice with this material. In addition, teachers should consult *Classical Outlook* for the annual articles written by the AP* Latin Chief Reader that discuss the grading of the AP* exam and include sample graded answers from actual student exams. The following test questions are not taken from old AP* exams (that material is copyrighted and is not available for use in commercial publications), but do, in large part, follow their style. These test questions should prove useful for both AP* and non-AP* Catullus students.

Poem 1

> Cui dono lepidum novum libellum
> arida modo pumice expolitum?
> Corneli, tibi: namque tu solebas
> meas esse aliquid putare nugas
> iam tum, cum ausus es unus Italorum   5
> omne aevum tribus explicare cartis
> doctis, Iuppiter, et laboriosis.

- Translate the passage above as literally as possible.

Poem 2

> Passer, deliciae meae puellae,
> quicum ludere, quem in sinu tenere,
> cui primum digitum dare appetenti
> et acris solet incitare morsus,

(lines 1–4)

- What trope or rhetorical figure is found in lines 2-4 above?

Poem 3

nam mellitus erat suamque norat
ipsam tam bene quam puella matrem,
nec sese a gremio illius movebat,
sed circumsiliens modo huc modo illuc
ad solam dominam usque pipiabat;   10
qui nunc it per iter tenebricosum
illuc, unde negant redire quemquam.

(lines 6–12)

- Who or what is being described in the passage above?
- Give two of his/her/its characteristics based on the lines above and cite the appropriate Latin.

Poem 4

Phaselus ille, quem videtis, hospites,
ait fuisse navium celerrimus,
neque ullius natantis impetum trabis
nequisse praeterire, sive palmulis
opus foret volare sive linteo.   5

- Of what trope or rhetorical figure is this an example?

Poem 5

dein mille altera, dein secunda centum

(line 8)

- Of what trope or rhetorical figure is this an example?

Poem 7

quam magnus numerus Libyssae harenae
lasarpiciferis iacet Cyrenis
oraclum Iovis inter aestuosi   5
et Batti veteris sacrum sepulcrum,
aut quam sidera multa, cum tacet nox,
furtivos hominum vident amores;

(lines 3–8)

- What poet is alluded to in these lines? Cite the Latin to support your answer.

Poem 8

Miser Catulle, desinas ineptire,
et quod vides perisse perditum ducas.

(lines 1–2)

- Translate the passage above as literally as possible.

- What case is "Miser" (line 1)?

- What mood is the verb "ducas" (line 2) and why?

Poem 10

Varus me meus ad suos amores
visum duxerat e foro otiosum,
scortillum, ut mihi tum repente visum est,
non sane illepidum neque invenustum.

(lines 1–4)

- Where else in the Catullan corpus does the issue of "leisure" (cf. line 2 above) appear? Give the Poem number(s) or briefly identify the poem (s).

huc ut venimus, incidere nobis   5
sermones varii: in quibus, quid esset
iam Bithynia; quo modo se haberet;
ecquonam mihi profuisset aere.

(lines 5–8)

- What is the significance of the place Bithynia in this poem? Where is it?

Poem 11

nec meum respectet, ut ante, amorem,
qui illius culpa cecidit velut prati
ultimi flos, praetereunte postquam
tactus aratro est.

(lines 21–24)

- What Latin word is the antecedent of "qui" (line 22)?

- What individual is the understood subject of the verb "respectet" (line 21)? (Do not just say he/she/it. Identify the individual.)

- What trope or rhetorical figure is introduced by "velut" (line 22)?

- Name the meter of this poem.

Poem 12

Marrucine Asini, manu sinistra
non belle uteris: in ioco atque vino
tollis lintea neglegentiorum.

(lines 1–3)

- What case is "manu" (line 1) and why?

Poem 13

sed contra accipies meros amores
seu quid suavius elegantiusve est: 10
nam unguentum dabo quod meae puellae
donarunt Veneres Cupidinesque,
quod tu cum olfacies, deos rogabis
totum ut te faciant, Fabulle, nasum.

(lines 9–14)

- Write out the metrical scansion of line 9 above.
- What case is "Veneres" (line 12)?
- What is the surprise in the last line?

Poem 14a

Ni te plus oculis meis amarem,
iucundissime Calve, munere isto
odissem te odio Vatiniano:

(lines 1–3)

- What grammatical condition is contained in these lines?

Poem 22

Suffenus iste, Vare, quem probe nosti,
homo est venustus et dicax et urbanus,
idemque longe plurimos facit versus.

(lines 1–3)

- Name one good quality and one bad quality Suffenus possesses based on these lines.

Poem 30

**si tu oblitus es, at di meminerunt, meminit Fides,
quae te ut paeniteat postmodo facti faciet tui.**

(lines 11–12)

- Fully identify the verb form "oblitus es" (line 11).
- What Latin word is the subject of "faciet" (line 12)?
- Give the case and number of "di" (line 11).

Poem 31

**salve, o venusta Sirmio, atque ero gaude
gaudente, vosque lucidae lacus undae
ridete quidquid est domi cachinnorum.**

(lines 12–14)

- Translate literally "atque ero gaude/gaudente."
- What case is "ero" (line 12) and why?
- What case is "domi" (line 14)?

Poem 35

**quae nunc, si mihi vera nuntiantur,
illum deperit impotente amore:
nam quo tempore legit incohatam
Dindymi dominam, ex eo misellae
ignes interiorem edunt medullam.**   15

(lines 11–15)

- Explain what has happened in the lines above.
- What trope or rhetorical figure appears in line 14 above?

Poem 36

nunc, o caeruleo creata ponto,
quae sanctum Idalium Uriosque apertos
quaeque Ancona Cnidumque harundinosam
colis quaeque Amathunta quaeque Golgos
quaeque Dyrrachium Hadriae tabernam,   15
acceptum face redditumque votum,
si non illepidum neque invenustum est.

(lines 11–17)

- Who is addressed in line 11 above?
- What is one place mentioned above that is located in Italy?

Poem 40

cum longa voluisti amare poena.

(line 8)

- Write out the metrical scansion of this line and name the meter.

Poem 43

Salve, nec minimo puella naso
nec bello pede nec nigris ocellis
nec longis digitis nec ore sicco
nec sane nimis elegante lingua.

(lines 1-4)

- What are two tropes or rhetorical figures found in these lines?

Poem 44

nam, Sestianus dum volo esse conviva,   10
orationem in Antium petitorem
plenam veneni et pestilentiae legi.

(lines 10–12)

- To what or whom do the words "Sestianus" and "Antium" refer?

Poem 45

Acmen Septimius suos amores
tenens in gremio "mea" inquit "Acme,
ni te perdite amo atque amare porro
omnes sum assidue paratus annos,
quantum qui pote plurimum perire,   5
solus in Libya Indiaque tosta
caesio ueniam obvius leoni."
hoc ut dixit, Amor sinistra ut ante
dextra sternuit approbationem.
  at Acme leviter caput reflectens   10
et dulcis pueri ebrios ocellos
illo purpureo ore saviata,
"sic," inquit "mea vita Septimille,
huic uni domino usque serviamus,
ut multo mihi maior acriorque   15
ignis mollibus ardet in medullis."
hoc ut dixit, Amor sinistra ut ante
dextra sternuit approbationem.
  nunc ab auspicio bono profecti
mutuis animis amant amantur.   20
unam Septimius misellus Acmen
mavult quam Syrias Britanniasque:
uno in Septimio fidelis Acme
facit delicias libidinesque.
quis ullos homines beatiores   25
vidit, quis venerem auspicatiorem?

- In a well-developed essay, discuss and support with specific references to the Latin the relationship between Septimius and Acme as portrayed in this poem. When supporting your answer with the Latin, make sure to cite line numbers AND translate or paraphrase the Latin to which you refer. Use evidence from throughout the passage, not just the beginning, middle, or end.

Poem 46

Iam ver egelidos refert tepores,
iam caeli furor aequinoctialis
iucundis Zephyri silescit auris.

(lines 1–3)

- List two signs of spring found in these lines.

Poem 49

Disertissime Romuli nepotum,
quot sunt quotque fuere, Marce Tulli,
quotque post aliis erunt in annis,

(lines 1–3)

• Who is addressed in these lines?

Poem 50

at defessa labore membra postquam
semimortua lectulo iacebant,   15
hoc, iucunde, tibi poema feci,
ex quo perspiceres meum dolorem.

(lines 14–17)

• Give the case of "poema" (line 16).
• Explain the use of the subjunctive in line 17 ("perspiceres").

Poem 51

lingua sed torpet, tenuis sub artus
flamma demanat, sonitu suopte   10
tintinant aures, gemina teguntur
   lumina nocte.

(lines 9–12)

• The symptoms described above are symptoms of what?
• What case is "lumina" (line 12)?

Poem 60

Num te leaena montibus Libystinis
aut Scylla latrans infima inguinum parte
tam mente dura procreavit ac taetra
ut supplicis vocem in novissimo casu
contemptam haberes, a nimis fero corde?   5

• Name one Greek or Latin author, other than Catullus, who refers to Scylla or uses the idea of "wild parentage"?

Poem 64 (lines 50–253)

quem procul ex alga maestis Minois ocellis

(line 60)

- "Minois" refers to whom?

quod tibi si sancti concesserit incola Itoni,

(line 228)

- The phrase "incola Itoni" refers to whom?
- In what genre, to which Poem 64 belongs, is allusive reference, as seen in the two examples above, common?

a misera, assiduis quam luctibus externavit

(line 71)

- Write out the metrical scansion of the line above.

"gnate mihi longe iucundior unice vita,

(line 215)

- What case is "vita" and why?

"sicine me patriis avectam, perfide, ab aris,
perfide, deserto liquisti in litore, Theseu?
sicine discedens neglecto numine divum,
immemor a! devota domum periuria portas?   135
nullane res potuit crudelis flectere mentis
consilium? tibi nulla fuit clementia praesto,
immite ut nostri vellet miserescere pectus?
at non haec quondam blanda promissa dedisti
voce mihi, non haec miseram sperare iubebas,   140
sed conubia laeta, sed optatos hymenaeos,
quae cuncta aerii discerpunt irrita venti.
nunc iam nulla viro iuranti femina credat,
nulla viri speret sermones esse fideles,
quis dum aliquid cupiens animus praegestit apisci,   145
nil metuunt iurare, nihil promittere parcunt;
sed simul ac cupidae mentis satiata libido est,
dicta nihil meminere, nihil periuria curant.
certe ego te in medio versantem turbine leti
eripui, et potius germanum amittere crevi   150
quam tibi fallaci supremo in tempore dessem.
pro quo dilaceranda feris dabor alitibusque
praeda, neque iniecta tumulabor mortua terra.
quaenam te genuit sola sub rupe leaena,
quod mare conceptum spumantibus exspuit undis,   155
quae Syrtis, quae Scylla rapax, quae vasta Charybdis,
talia qui reddis pro dulci praemia vita?
si tibi non cordi fuerant conubia nostra,
saeva quod horrebas prisci praecepta parentis,
attamen in vestras potuisti ducere sedes,   160
quae tibi iucundo famularer serva labore,
candida permulcens liquidis vestigia lymphis,
purpureave tuum consternens veste cubile.

• The passage above is a selection from Poem 64 containing some of Ariadne's speech to Theseus.
In a well-developed essay, discuss and support with specific references to the Latin how
Ariadne views herself, Theseus, and her current condition in this selection. When
supporting your answer with the Latin, make sure to cite line numbers AND translate
or paraphrase the Latin to which you refer. Use evidence from throughout the passage,
not just the beginning, middle, or end.

Poem 65

sed tamen in tantis maeroribus, Hortale, mitto   15
  haec expressa tibi carmina Battiadae,
ne tua dicta vagis nequiquam credita ventis
  effluxisse meo forte putes animo,
ut missum sponsi furtivo munere malum
  procurrit casto virginis e gremio,   20
quod miserae oblitae molli sub veste locatum,
  dum adventu matris prosilit, excutitur,
atque illud prono praeceps agitur decursu,
  huic manat tristi conscius ore rubor.

(lines 15–24)

- Give a literal translation of lines 19–24.

Poem 68 (lines 1–40)

Quod mihi fortuna casuque oppressus acerbo
  conscriptum hoc lacrimis mittis epistolium,
naufragum ut eiectum spumantibus aequoris undis
  sublevem et a mortis limine restituam,
quem neque sancta Venus molli requiescere somno   5
  desertum in lecto caelibe perpetitur,
nec veterum dulci scriptorum carmine Musae
  oblectant, cum mens anxia pervigilat:
id gratum est mihi, me quoniam tibi dicis amicum,
  muneraque et Musarum hinc petis et Veneris.   10

(lines 1–10)

- To what circumstances does the image of shipwreck refer in lines 3–4?
- To what does "id" (line 9) refer?

...frater adempte mihi,

(line 20)

- In what other poem in the Student Text do these same words appear?

cuius ego interitu tota de mente fugavi   25
    haec studia atque omnes delicias animi.
quare, quod scribis Veronae turpe Catullo
    esse, quod hic quisquis de meliore nota
frigida deserto tepefactet membra cubili,
    id, Manli, non est turpe, magis miserum est.

(lines 25–30)

• What case is "Veronae" (line 27)?

• Whose death is referred to in line 25?

Poem 69

Noli admirari, quare tibi femina nulla,
    Rufe, velit tenerum supposuisse femur,
non si illam rarae labefactes munere vestis
    aut perluciduli deliciis lapidis.
laedit te quaedam mala fabula, qua tibi fertur   5
    valle sub alarum trux habitare caper.
hunc metuunt omnes, neque mirum: nam mala valde est
    bestia, nec quicum bella puella cubet.
quare aut crudelem nasorum interfice pestem,
    aut admirari desine cur fugiunt.   10

• Name the meter of this poem and write out the metrical scansion for lines 7–8.

• Explain Rufus' problem. Cite the Latin in the poem that supports your answer and translate it.

Poem 70

Nulli se dicit mulier mea nubere malle
    quam mihi, non si se Iuppiter ipse petat.
dicit; sed mulier cupido quod dicit amanti,
    in vento et rapida scribere oportet aqua.

• Explain the use of the subjunctive found in "petat" (line 1).

• To whom or what does "se" (line 1) refer?

• Give the case of "amanti" (line 3).

Poem 72

dilexi tum te non tantum ut vulgus amicam,
  sed pater ut gnatos diligit et generos.

(lines 3–4)

- What are the two kinds of love found in these lines?

Poem 76

non iam illud quaero, contra ut me diligat illa,
  aut, quod non potis est, esse pudica velit:
ipse valere opto et taetrum hunc deponere morbum.   25
  o di, reddite mi hoc pro pietate mea.

(lines 23–26)

- What is the sense of "pudica" in line 24?
- What is it that the speaker says he no longer wants (lines 23-24)?
- What does the speaker say he wants (line 25)?

Poem 77

Rufe mihi frustra ac nequiquam credite amice
  (frustra? immo magno cum pretio atque malo),
sicine subrepsti mi atque intestina perurens
  ei misero eripuisti omnia nostra bona?
eripuisti, eheu nostrae crudele venenum   5
  vitae, eheu nostrae pestis amicitiae.

- What case is "venenum" (line 5)?
- Give the case, number, and gender of "omnia" (line 4).

Poem 84

Ionios fluctus, postquam illuc Arrius isset,
  iam non Ionios esse sed Hionios.

(lines 11–12)

- What is Arrius' problem? What Latin words in these lines point to his problem?

Poem 85

Odi et amo. quare id faciam, fortasse requiris.
    nescio, sed fieri sentio et excrucior.

- How many active verb forms are there in this two-line poem? Which verb, in a sense, lies at the "crossroads" between active and passive?
- Explain in a few sentences the significance of activity and passivity in the social and cultural context of Roman sexuality.

Poem 86

totum illud "formosa" nego: nam nulla venustas,
    nulla in tam magno est corpore mica salis.

(lines 3–4)
- Why do modern editors put the word "formosa" within quotation marks?

Poem 87

Nulla potest mulier tantum se dicere amatam
    vere, quantum a me Lesbia amata mea es.
nulla fides ullo fuit umquam in foedere tanta,
    quanta in amore tuo ex parte reperta mea est.

- What part of speech is "vere" in line 2 of the poem above?

Poem 96

Si quicquam mutis gratum acceptumve sepulcris
    accidere a nostro, Calve, dolore potest,
quo desiderio veteres renovamus amores
    atque olim missas flemus amicitias,
certe non tanto mors immatura dolori est   5
    Quintiliae, quantum gaudet amore tuo.

- Who is Quintilia? Why does that matter for the reading of this poem?

Poem 101

accipe fraterno multum manantia fletu,
    atque in perpetuum, frater, ave atque vale.

(lines 9–10)

• What actions does the speaker take in these lines?

Poem 109

Iucundum, mea vita, mihi proponis: amorem
    hunc nostrum inter nos perpetuum usque fore.

(lines 1–2)

• Explain the form of "fore" (line 2).

Poem 116

qui te lenirem nobis, neu conarere

(line 3)

• What is metrically unusual about this line?

ANNOTATED BIBLIOGRAPHY

The scholarship on Catullus is vast. I have tried to emphasize in this select bibliography scholarship written in English that will be useful for readers of the AP* syllabus. The emphasis in the selections is on recent articles and books that will allow the reader to become aware of current critical thought on Catullus.

Annotation, where provided, is for the benefit of the Latin teacher teaching the poems in *Writing Passion: A Catullus Reader*.

Commentaries

Arnold, Bruce, Andrew Aronson, and Gilbert Lawall. *Love and Betrayal: A Catullus Reader*. Upper Saddle River, N.J.: Prentice Hall, 2000.

——. *Love and Betrayal: A Catullus Reader—Teacher's Guide*. Upper Saddle River, N.J.: Prentice Hall, 2000.

Aronson, A., and Robert Boughner. *Catullus and Horace: Selections from Their Lyric Poetry*. White Plains, N.Y.: Longman, 1988.

Aronson, Andrew. *Catullus and Horace: A Selection with Facing Vocabularies and Notes*. Amherst, Mass.: New England Classical Newsletter Publications, 1989–90.

Bender, Henry V., and Phyllis Young Forsyth. *Catullus—Student Text*. Wauconda, Ill.: Bolchazy-Carducci Publishers, 1997.

Fordyce, C. J. *Catullus*. Oxford: Oxford University Press, 1961. (USEFUL EDITION FOR THE TEACHER TO CONSULT, ALTHOUGH IT DOES NOT CONTAIN ALL OF CATULLUS' POEMS.)

Forsyth, Phyllis Young. *The Poems of Catullus—A Teaching Text*. Lanham, Md.: University Press of America, 1986. (TEXT AND NOTES FOR ALL OF CATULLUS' POEMS. USEFUL FOR THE TEACHER TO CONSULT.)

Garrison, Daniel H. *The Student's Catullus*. Second Edition. Norman, Okla. and London: University of Oklahoma Press, 1995. (TEXT AND NOTES FOR ALL OF CATULLUS' POEMS. USEFUL FOR THE TEACHER TO CONSULT.)

Goold, G. P. *Catullus*. Bristol: Bristol Classical Press, 1983. (INCLUDES A TRANSLATION)

Merrill, Elmer T. *Catullus*. Boston: Ginn, 1893.

Quinn, Kenneth. *Catullus—The Poems*. Second Edition. London: Macmillan, 1973. (TEXT AND NOTES FOR ALL OF CATULLUS' POEMS. USEFUL FOR THE TEACHER TO CONSULT.)

* AP is a registered trademark of the College Entrance Examination Board, which was not involved in the production of, and does not endorse, this product.

Thomson, D. F. S. *Catullus: Edited with a Textual and Interpretative Commentary*. Toronto: University of Toronto Press, 1997. (THIS IS THE LATEST SCHOLARLY EDITION AND COMMENTARY ON THE POEMS. HARD-COVER EDITION EXPENSIVE; PAPERBACK [2003] REASONABLE. EXCELLENT RESOURCE FOR THE TEACHER WHO WANTS TO BE CURRENT ON CATULLAN SCHOLARSHIP.)

Translations

Gaisser, Julia Haig. *Catullus in English*: London: Penguin, 2001.

Lee, Guy. *The Complete Poems of Catullus*. Oxford: Oxford University Press, 1998.

Martin, Charles. *The Poems of Catullus*. Baltimore and London: Johns Hopkins University Press, 1990. (USEFUL LIVELY, NOT NECESSARILY LITERAL, TRANSLATIONS.)

Michie, J. *The Poems of Catullus*. London: Duckworth, 1990.

Rabinowitz, Jacob. *Gaius Valerius Catullus' Complete Poetic Works*. Woodstock, Conn.: Spring Publications, 1991.

Whigham, Peter. *The Poems of Catullus*. London: Penguin, 1966.

Listening Materials

Novák, Jan. *Schola Cantans*. Cassette, libretto, and musical score. Wauconda, Ill.: Bolchazy-Carducci Publishers, 1998. (INCLUDES POEMS OF CATULLUS SET TO MUSIC)

Orff, Carl. *Catulli Carmina*. (MUSICAL PIECE INCORPORATING SELECTIONS FROM CATULLUS, AVAILABLE UNDER VARIOUS MUSIC LABELS)

Sonkowsky, Robert P. *The Living Voice of Latin Literature: Selections from Catullus and Horace*. Booklet and two cassettes. Guilford, Conn.: Jeffrey Norton, 1984. Distributed by Bolchazy-Carducci Publishers, Wauconda, Ill.

St. Louis Chamber Chorus. *Rome's Golden Poets*. Limited edition CD. Wauconda, Ill.: Bolchazy-Carducci Publishers, 1999. (INCLUDES POEMS OF CATULLUS SET TO MUSIC)

Books on Catullus and Background to Catullus

Adler, Eve. *Catullan Self-Revelation*. New York: Arno Press, 1981.

Arkins, Brian. *Sexuality in Catullus*. Hildesheim: Georg Olms, 1982.

Dettmer, Helena. *Love by the Numbers: Form and Meaning in the Poetry of Catullus*. New York: Peter Lang, 1997.

Dixon, Suzanne. *Reading Roman Women*. London: Duckworth, 2001. (CHAPTER 9, ON THE "MYTH AND REALITY" OF CLODIA/LESBIA, USEFUL FOR READERS OF CATULLUS AND CICERO'S *PRO CAELIO*.)

Edwards, Catharine. *The Politics of Immorality in Ancient Rome*. Cambridge: Cambridge University Press, 1993. (USEFUL ON ISSUES OF GENDER AND SEXUALITY.)

Ferguson, John. *Catullus (Greek and Roman Surveys in the Classics 20)*. Oxford: Clarendon Press, 1988.

———. *Catullus*. Lawrence, Kans.: Coronado Press, 1985.

Fitzgerald, William. *Catullan Provocations: Lyric Poetry and the Drama of Position*. Berkeley: University of California Press, 1995. (CHAPTER 2 USEFUL ON THE "EROTICS OF POETRY".)

Gaisser, Julia. *Catullus and His Renaissance Readers*. Oxford: Clarendon Press, 1993.

Greene, Ellen. *The Erotics of Domination: Male Desire and the Mistress in Latin Love Poetry*. Baltimore and London: Johns Hopkins University Press, 1998.

Habinek, Thomas. *The Politics of Latin Literature: Writing, Identity and Empire in Ancient Rome*. Princeton: Princeton University Press, 1998.

Havelock, Eric. *The Lyric Genius of Catullus*. Oxford: Blackwell, 1939.

Janan, Micaela. *When The Lamp Is Shattered: Desire and Narrative in Catullus*. Carbondale, Ill.: Southern Illinois University Press, 1994.

Jenkyns, Richard. *Three Classical Poets: Sappho, Catullus and Juvenal*. London: Duckworth, 1982.

Johnson, W. Ralph. *The Idea of Lyric*. Berkeley: University of California Press, 1982.

Kresic, Stephanus, ed. *Contemporary Literary Hermeneutics and Interpretation of Classical Texts*. Ottawa: Ottawa University Press, 1981. (CONTAINS ARTICLES ON CATULLUS 8 BY S. KRESIC, P. J. McCORMICK AND H.-G. GADAMER)

Lyne, R. O. A. M. *The Latin Love Poets*. Oxford: Clarendon Press, 1980.

Martin, Charles. *Catullus*. New Haven and London: Yale University Press, 1992.

McCarren, Vincent P. *A Critical Concordance to Catullus*. Leiden: Brill, 1977.

Miller, Paul Allen. *Lyric Texts and Lyric Consciousness: The Birth of a Genre From Archaic Greece to Augustan Rome*. London and New York: Routledge, 1994. (CHAPTER 6 USEFUL ON SAPPHO AND CATULLUS IN POEM 51.)

Newman, J. K. *Roman Catullus and the Modification of the Alexandrian Sensibility*. Hildesheim: Weidmann, 1990.

Putnam, Michael C. J. *Essays on Latin Lyric, Elegy, and Epic*. Princeton: Princeton University Press, 1982.

Quinn, Kenneth. *The Catullan Revolution*. Second Edition. London: Bristol Classical Press, 1999.

Ross, David O. *Style and Tradition in Catullus*. Cambridge: Harvard University Press, 1969.

Skinner, Marilyn B. *Catullus' Passer: The Arrangement of the Book of Polymetric Poems*. New York: Arno Press, 1981.

Small, Stuart. *Catullus: A Reader's Guide to the Poems*. Lanham, Md.: University Press of America, 1983.

Sullivan, J. P., ed. *Critical Essays on Roman Literature: Elegy and Lyric*. Cambridge: Harvard University Press, 1962.

Treggiari, Susan. *Roman Marriage*. Oxford: Clarendon Press, 1991.

Wheeler, A. L. *Catullus and the Traditions of Ancient Poetry* (1934). Berkeley: University of California Press, 1964.

Williams, Gordon. *The Nature of Roman Poetry*. Oxford: Oxford University Press, 1983.

Wiseman, T. P. *Catullus and His World*. Cambridge: Cambridge University Press, 1985. (GOOD GENERAL BACKGROUND ON CATULLUS AND HIS CONTEXT.)

——. *Catullan Questions*. Leicester: Leicester University Press, 1969.

Witke, Charles. *Enarratio Catulliana*. Leiden: Brill, 1968.

Wray, David. *Catullus and the Poetics of Manhood*. Cambridge: Cambridge University Press, 2001.

Selected Articles on Catullus

Arkins, Brian. "Caelius and Rufus in Catullus." *Philologus* 127 (1983): 306–11.

Clausen, Wendell. "Cicero and the New Poetry." *Harvard Studies in Classical Philology* 90 (1986): 159–70.

——. "Catullus and Callimachus." *Harvard Studies in Classical Philology* 74 (1970): 86–94.

——. "Callimachus and Latin Poetry." *Greek, Roman and Byzantine Studies* 5 (1964): 181–96.

Commager, Steele. "Notes on Some Poems of Catullus." *Harvard Studies in Classical Philology* 70 (1965): 83–110.

Crowther, N. B. "Parthenius and Roman Poetry." *Mnemosyne* 29 (1976): 66–71.

——. "Catullus and the Traditions of Latin Poetry." *Classical Philology* 66 (1971): 246–49.

——. "οἱ νεώτεροι, *poetae novi*, and *cantores Euphorionis*." *Classical Quarterly* 20 (1970): 322–27.

Duclos, G. S. "Catullus 11: Atque in perpetuum, Lesbia, ave atque vale." *Arethusa* 9 (1976): 76–89.

Elder, J. P. "Notes on Some Conscious and Unconscious Elements in Catullus' Poetry." *Harvard Studies in Classical Philology* 60 (1951): 101–36.

Forsyth, Phyllis Young. "Catullus: The Mythic Persona." *Latomus* 35 (1976): 556–66.

Fowler, Don. "Postmodernism, Romantic Irony and Classical Closure." In *Modern Critical Theory and Classical Literature*, edited by I. De Jong and J. P. Sullivan. Leiden: Brill, 1994: 231–56.

Fredricksmeyer, Ernst. "The Beginning and the End of Catullus' *Longus Amor*." *Symbolae Osloenses* 58 (1983): 63–88.

Gaffney, G. Edward. "*Severitati Respondere*: Character Drawing in the *Pro Caelio* and Catullus' *Carmina*." *Classical Journal* 90 (1995): 423–31.

Greene, Ellen. "The Catullan Ego: Fragmentation and the Erotic Self." *American Journal of Philology* 116 (1995): 77–93.

Grimaldi, W. M. A. "The Lesbia Love Lyrics." *Classical Philology* 60 (1965): 87–95.

Hubbard, Thomas K. "The Catullan Libellus." *Philologus* 127 (1983): 218–37.

Konstan, David. "Two Kinds of Love in Catullus." *Classical Journal* 68 (1972): 102–06.

Lateiner, D. "Obscenity in Catullus." *Ramus* 6 (1977): 16–32.

Lyne, R. O. A. M. "The Neoteric Poets." *Classical Quarterly* 28 (1978): 167–87.

Minyard, J. D. "The Source of the *Catulli Veronensis Liber*." *Classical World* 81 (1988): 343–53.

Putnam, M. C. J. "The Future of Catullus." *The Transactions and Proceedings of the American Philological Association* 113 (1983): 243–62.

Rankin, H. D. "The Progress of Pessimism in Catullus, Poems 2–11." *Latomus* 31 (1972): 744–51.

———. "Clodia II." *L'Antiquité Classique* 38 (1969) 501–06.

Rubino, Carl. "The Erotic World of Catullus." *Classical World* 68 (1975): 289–97.

Santirocco, Matthew. ed. "Special Section on Teaching Catullus." *Classical World* 95 (2002): 413–438. (CONTRIBUTIONS BY HENRY BENDER, DANIEL GARRISON, JUDITH HALLETT, PAUL ALLEN MILLER, LEE PEARCY, MARILYN SKINNER.)

Seager, R. "*Venustus, Lepidus, Bellus, Salsus*: Notes on the Language of Catullus." *Latomus* 33 (1974): 891–94.

Segal, Charles. "The Order of Catullus, Poems 2–11." *Latomus* 27 (1968): 306–21.

Selden, D. "Ceveat lector: Catullus and the rhetoric of performance." In *Innovations of Antiquity*, edited by R. Hexter and D. Selden. New York: Routledge (1992): 461–512.

Skinner, Marilyn B. "*Ego mulier*: The Construction of Male Sexuality in Catullus." *Helios* 20 (1993): 107–30.

———. "Clodia Metelli." *Transactions and Proceedings of the American Philological Association* 113 (1983): 273–82.

———. "Pretty Lesbius." *Transactions and Proceedings of the American Philological Association* 112 (1982): 197–208.

———. "Parasites and Strange Bedfellows: A Study in Catullus' Political Imagery." *Ramus* 8 (1980): 137–52.

Tatum, W. Jeffrey. "Friendship, Politics, and Literature in Catullus: Poems 1, 65 and 66, 116." *Classical Quarterly* 47 (1997) 482–500.

Vinson, Martha. "Party Politics and the Language of Love in the Lesbia Poems of Catullus." In *Collection Latomus: Studies in Latin Literature and Roman History* 6, edited by C. Deroux. Brussels: Latomus, 1992: 163–80.

———. "And Baby Makes Three? Parental Imagery in the Lesbia poems of Catullus." *Classical Journal* 85 (1989–90): 47–53.

Wiltshire, Susan F. "Catullus Venustus." *Classical World* 70 (1977): 319–26.

References Works

Abrams, M. H. *A Glossary of Literary Terms*. Seventh Edition. Fort Worth, Tex.: Harcourt, Brace, Jovanovich, 1998. (USEFUL GLOSSARY OF IMPORTANT LITERARY TERMS)

Adams, J. N. *The Latin Sexual Vocabulary*. Baltimore: Johns Hopkins University Press, 1982. (ESSENTIAL RESOURCE FOR SEXUAL WORDS IN LATIN)

Halporn, James W., Martin Ostwald, and Thomas G. Rosenmeyer. *The Meters of Greek and Latin Poetry*. Revised Edition. Indianapolis: Hackett Publishing Company, 1994.

Holoka, J. P. *Gaius Valerius Catullus: A Systematic Bibliography*. New York and London: Garland, 1985.

Preminger, Alex. *The New Princeton Encyclopedia of Poetry and Poetics*. Third Edition. Princeton: Princeton University Press, 1993. (USEFUL FOR DISCUSSIONS OF GENERAL POETIC TERMS AND ISSUES)

Material Relevant to Specific Poems in the AP* Syllabus

(See also "Selected Articles on Catullus" [above] as well as relevant sections of the books on Catullus [above]).

Poem 1

Batstone, William. "Dry Pumice and the Programmatic Language of Catullus 1." *Classical Philology* 93 (1998): 126–35.

Rauk, John. "Time and History in Catullus 1." *Classical World* 90 (1997): 319–32.

Poem 2

Brotherton, B. "Catullus' Carmen II." *Classical Philology* 21 (1926): 361–63.

Genovese, E. N. "Symbolism in the Passer Poems." *Maia* 26 (1974): 121–25.

Giangrande, G. "Catullus' Lyrics on the Passer." *Museum Philologum Londiniense* 1 (1975): 137–46.

Hooper, R. W. "In Defence of Catullus' Dirty Sparrow." *Greece and Rome* 32 (1985): 162–78.

Jocelyn, H. D. "On Some Unnecessarily Indecent Interpretations of Catullus 2 and 3." *American Journal of Philology* 101 (1980): 421–41.

Jones, Julian Ward, Jr. "Catullus' *Passer* as *Passer*." *Greece and Rome* 45 (1998): 188–94.

Nadeau, Yvan. "Catullus' Sparrow, Martial, Juvenal and Ovid." *Latomus* 43 (1984): 861–68.

Thomas, Richard F. "Sparrows, Hares, and Doves: a Catullan Metaphor." *Helios* 20 (1993): 131–42.

Poem 3

Akbar Khan, H.. "A Note on the Expression *solum...nosse* in Catullus." *Classical Philology* 62 (1967): 34–36.

Elerick, Charles. "On Translating Catullus 3." *Scholia* 2 (1993): 90–96.

Poem 4

Coleman, K. M. "The Persona of Catullus' *Phaselus*." *Greece and Rome* 28 (1981): 68–72.

Copley, F. O. "Catullus 4: The World of the Poem." *Transactions and Proceedings of the American Philological Association* 89 (1958): 9–13.

Griffith, J. G. "Catullus Poem 4: A Neglected Interpretation Revived." *Phoenix* 37 (1983): 123–28.

Putnam, Michael C. J. "Catullus' Journey (Carm. 4)." *Classical Philology* 57 (1962): 10–19. (Reprinted in Putnam, *Essays*. Cf. book section of this bibliography.)

Poem 5

Commager, Steele. "The Structure of Catullus 5." *Classical Journal* 59 (1964): 361–64.

Fredricksmeyer, Ernst. A. "Observations on Catullus 5." *American Journal of Philology* 91 (1970): 431–45.

Grimm, R. E. "Catullus 5 Again." *Classical Journal* 59 (1963): 16–21.

Grummel, W. C. "Vivamus, mea Lesbia." *Classical Bulletin* 31 (1954): 19–21.

Pratt, N. T. "The Numerical Catullus 5." *Classical Philology* 51 (1956): 99–100.

Segal, Charles. "Catullus 5 and 7: A Study in Complementaries." *American Journal of Philology* 89 (1968): 284–301.

Poem 7

Arkins, Brian. "Catullus 7." *L'Antiquité Classique* 48 (1979): 630–35.

Johnston, Patricia A. "Love and Laserpicium in Catullus 7." *Classical Philology* 88 (1993): 328–29.

Moorhouse, A. C. "Two Adjectives in Catullus 7." *American Journal of Philology* 84 (1963): 417–18.

Segal (see Poem 5).

Segal, Charles. "More Alexandrianism in Catullus VII?" *Mnemosyne* 27 (1974): 139–43.

Poem 8

Akbar Khan, H. "Style and Meaning in Catullus' Eighth Poem." *Latomus* 27 (1968): 556–74.

Connor, P. J. "Catullus 8: The Lover's Conflict." *Antichthon* 8 (1974): 93–96.

Dyson, M., "Catullus 8 and 76." *Classical Quarterly* 23 (1973): 127–43.

Moritz, L. A. "Miser Catulle: A Postscript." *Greece and Rome* 13 (1966): 156–57.

Rowland, R. L. *"Miser Catulle*: An Interpretation of the Eighth Poem of Catullus." *Greece and Rome* 13 (1966): 16–21.

Schmiel, R. "The Structure of Catullus 8: A History of Interpretation." *Classical Journal* 86 (1990–91): 158–66.

Skinner, Marilyn B. "Catullus 8: The Comic Amator as Eiron." *Classical Journal* 66 (1971): 298–305.

Swanson, R. A. "The Humor of Catullus 8." *Classical Journal* 58 (1963): 193–96.

Poem 10

Braund, David C. "The Politics of Catullus 10: Memmius, Caesar, and the Bithynians." *Hermathena* 160 (1996): 46–57.

Nielsen, Rosemary M. "Catullus and *Sal* (Poem 10)." *L'Antiquité Classique* 56 (1987): 148–61.

Sedgwick, W. B. "Catullus X: A Rambling Commentary." *Greece and Rome* 16 (1947): 108–14.

Skinner, Marilyn B. *"Ut decuit cinaediorem*: Power, Gender and Urbanity in Catullus 10." *Helios* 16 (1989): 7–23.

Poem 11

Ancona (see Poem 51).

Blodgett, E. D., and R. M. Nielsen. "Mask and Figure in Catullus, Carmen 11." *Revue Belge de Philologie et Histoire* 54 (1986): 22–31.

Bright, D. F. "*Non Bona Dicta*: Catullus' Poetry of Separation." *Quaderni Urbinati di Cultura Classica* 21 (1976): 106–19.

Forsyth, Phyllis Y. "The Thematic Unity of Catullus 11." *Classical World* 84 (1990–91): 457–64.

Fredricksmeyer, Ernst A. "Method and Interpretation: Catullus 11." *Helios* 20 (1993): 89–105.

Heath, John R. "Catullus 11: Along for the Ride." In *Collection Latomus: Studies in Latin Literature and Roman History* 5, edited by C. Deroux. Brussells: Latomus, 1989: 98–116.

Mayer, R. "Catullus' Divorce." *Classical Quarterly* 33 (1983): 297–98.

Putnam, Michael C. J. "Catullus 11: The Ironies of Integrity." *Ramus* 3 (1974): 70–86. (Reprinted in Putnam, *Essays*. Cf. book section of this bibliography.)

Sweet, David. "Catullus 11: A Study in Perspective." *Latomus* 46 (1987): 510–26.

Poem 12

Forsyth, Phyllis Y. "Gifts and Giving: Catullus 12–14." *Classical World* 79 (1985): 571–74.

Nappa, Christopher. "Place Settings: *Convivium*, Contrast, and Persona in Catullus 12 and 13." *American Journal of Philology* 119 (1998): 386–97.

Poem 13

Arkins, Brian. "Poem 13 of Catullus." *Symbolae Osloenses* 54 (1979): 71–80.

Bernstein, W. H. "A Sense of Taste: Catullus 13." *Classical Journal* 80 (1985): 127–30.

Case, Beau David. "'Guess who's coming to dinner?': a note on Catullus 13." *Latomus* 54 (1995): 876–76.

Dettmer, Helena. "Catullus 13: A Nose is a Nose." *Syllecta Classica* 1 (1989): 76–85.

———. "*Meros Amores*: a Note on Catullus 13,9." *Quaderni Urbinati di Cultura Classica* 52 (1986): 87–91.

Fitts, R. L. "Reflections on Catullus 13." *Classical World* 76 (1982): 41–42.

Forsyth (see Poem 12).

Hallett, J. P. "Divine Unction: Some Further Thoughts on Catullus 13." *Latomus* 37 (1978): 747–48.

Helm, J. J. "Poetic Structure and Humor: Catullus 13." *Classical World* 74 (1980–81): 213–17.

Littman, R. J. "The Unguent of Venus: Catullus 13." *Latomus* 36 (1977): 123–28.

Marcovich, Miroslav. "Catullus 13 and Philodemus 23." *Quaderni Urbinati di Cultura Classica* 40 (1982): 131–38.

Nappa (see Poem 12).

Nielsen, R. M., and E. D. Blodgett. "Catullus' *Cena*: 'I'll Tell You of More, and Lie, So You Will Come." *Revue Belge de Philologie et Histoire* 69 (1991): 87–100.

Richlin, Amy. "Systems of Food Imagery in Catullus." *Classical World* 81 (1988): 356–63.

Vessey, D. W. T. C. "Thoughts on Two Poems of Catullus: 13 and 30." *Latomus* 30 (1971): 46–55.

Witke, Charles. "Catullus 13." *Classical Philology* 75 (1980): 326–31.

Poem 14

Bower, E. W. "Some Technical Terms in Roman Education." *Hermes* 89 (1961): 462–77.

Poem 22

Watson, Lindsay. "Rustic Suffenus (Catullus 22) and Literary Rusticity." In *Papers of the Leeds International Latin Seminar: Volume 6,* edited by F. Cairns and M. Heath. Leeds: Leeds University Press, 1990: 13–33.

Poem 30

Thom, Sjarlene. "Crime and punishment in Catullus 30." *Akroterion* 38 (1993): 51–60.

Poem 31

Baker, R. J. "Catullus and Sirmio." *Mnemosyne* 36 (1983): 316–23.

Cairns, F. "Venusta Sirmio: Catullus 31." In *Quality and Pleasure in Latin Poetry,* edited by T. Woodman and D. West. Cambridge: Cambridge University Press, 1974: 1–17.

McCaughey, J. "The Mind Lays By Its Trouble: Catullus 31." *Arion* 9 (1970): 362–65.

Nielsen (see Poem 9).

Witke, Charles. "Verbal Art in Catullus 31." *American Journal of Philology* 93 (1972): 239–51.

Poem 35

Akbar Khan, H. "Catullus 35 and the Things Poetry Can Do to You." *Hermes* 102 (1974): 476–90.

Copley, Frank. "Catullus 35." *American Journal of Philology* 74 (1953): 149–60.

Fisher, J. M. "Catullus 35." *Classical Philology* 66 (1971): 1–5.

Foster, Jonathan. "Poetry and Friendship: Catullus 35." *Liverpool Classical Monthly* 19 (1994): 114–21.

Fredricksmeyer, Ernst A. "Catullus to Caecilius on Good Poetry." *American Journal of Philology* 106 (1985): 213–21.

Solodow, J. P. "Forms of Literary Criticism in Catullus: Polymetric vs. Epigram." *Classical Philology* 84 (1989): 312–19.

Poem 36

Clarke, G. W. "The Burning of Books and Catullus 36." *Latomus* 27 (1968): 576–80.

Comfort, H. "An Interpretation of Catullus XXXVI." *Classical Philology* 24 (1929): 176–82.

Morgan, M. Gwyn. "Catullus and the Annales Volusi." *Quaderni Urbinati di Cultura Classica* 4 (1980): 59–67.

Østerud, S. "Sacrifice and Bookburning in Catullus' Poem 36." *Hermes* 106 (1978): 138–55.

Solodow (see Poem 35).

Poem 40

Forsyth, P. Y. "The Lady and the Poem: Catullus 36–42." *Classical Journal* 80 (1984): 24–26.

Hendrickson, G. L. "Archilochus and Catullus." *Classical Philology* 20 (1925): 156–57.

Poem 43

Rankin, H. D. "Catullus and the Beauty of Lesbia (Poems 43, 86, and 51)." *Latomus* 35 (1976): 3–11.

Skinner, Marilyn B. "Ameana, Puella Defututa." *Classical Journal* 74 (1978–79): 110–14.

Poem 44

de Angeli, E. S. "A Literary Chill: Catullus 44." *Classical World* 62 (1969): 354–56.

George, David. "Catullus 44: The Vulnerability of Wanting to be Included." *American Journal of Philology* 112 (1991): 247–50.

Jones, C. P. "Parody in Catullus 44." *Hermes* 92 (1968): 379–83.

Poem 45

Akbar Khan, H. "Catullus 45: What Sort of Irony?" *Latomus* 27 (1968): 3–12.

Frueh, Edward. "*Sinistra ut ante dextra*: Reading Catullus 45." *Classical World* 84 (1990–91): 16–21.

Gratwick, Adrian S. "Those Sneezes: Catullus 45.8–9, 17–18." *Classical Philology* 87 (1992): 234–40.

Kitzinger, Rachel. "Reading Catullus 45." *Classical Journal* 87 (1991–92): 209–17.

Newton, Rick. "Acme and Septimius Recounted: Catullus 45." *Syllecta Classica* 7 (1996): 99–105.

Nielsen, R. "Catullus 45 and Horace *Odes* 3.9: The Glass House." *Ramus* 6 (1977): 132–38.

Ross, D. O. "Style and Content in Catullus 45." *Classical Philology* 60 (1965): 256–59.

Singleton, D. "Form and Irony in Catullus 45." *Greece and Rome* 18 (1971): 181–87.

Williams, M. F. "Amor's Head-Cold (*frigus* in Catullus 45)." *Classical Journal* 83 (1988): 128–32.

Poem 46

Simpson, C. J., and Barbara G. Simpson. "Catullus 46." *Latomus* 48 (1989): 76–85.

Poem 49

Basson, W. P. "The Riddle of Catullus 49: Some Notes on its Interpretation." *Acta Classica* 23 (1980): 46–52.

Batstone, William. "Logic, Rhetoric and Poesis." *Helios* 20 (1993): 143–72.

Fredricksmeyer, Ernst. "Catullus 49, Cicero, and Caesar." *Classical Philology* 68 (1973): 268–78.

Laughton, E. "Disertissime Romuli nepotum." *Classical Philology* 65 (1970): 1–7.

McDermott, W. C. "Cicero and Catullus." *Wiener Studien* 14 (1980): 76–82.

Svavarsson, Svavar Hrafn. "On Catullus 49." *Classical Journal* 95 (1999): 131–38.

Tatum, W. Jeffrey. "Catullus' Criticism of Cicero in Poem 49." *Transactions and Proceedings of the American Philological Association* 118 (1988): 179–84.

Thomson, D. F. S. "Catullus and Cicero: Poetry and the Criticism of Poetry." *Classical World* 60 (1967): 226–30.

Wormell, D. E. W. "Catullus 49." *Phoenix* 17 (1963): 59–60.

Poem 50

Burgess, D. L. "Catullus c. 50: the Exchange of Poetry." *American Journal of Philology* 107 (1986): 576–86.

Finamore, John F. "Catullus 50 and 51: Friendship, Love, and *Otium*." *Classical World* 78 (1984): 11–19.

Scott, W. C. "Catullus and Calvus (Cat. 50)." *Classical Philology* 64 (1969): 169–73.

Segal, Charles. "Catullan *otiosi*—The Lover and the Poet." *Greece and Rome* 17 (1970): 26–31.

Williams, Mark F. "Catullus 50 and the Language of Friendship." *Latomus* 47 (1988): 69–73.

Poem 51

Ancona, Ronnie. "The Untouched Self: Sapphic and Catullan Muses in Horace *Odes* 1.22." In *Cultivating the Muse: Struggles for Power and Inspiration in Classical Literature*, edited by Efrossini Spentzou and Don Fowler. Oxford: Oxford University Press, 2002: 161–86.

Finamore (see Poem 50).

Frank, R. I. "Catullus 51: *Otium* versus *Virtus*." *Transactions and Proceedings of the American Philological Association* 99 (1968): 233–39.

Fredricksmeyer, Ernst. "On the Unity of Catullus 51." *Transactions and Proceedings of the American Philological Association* 96 (1965): 153–63.

Greene, Ellen. "Re-Figuring the Feminine Voice: Catullus Translating Sappho." *Arethusa* 32 (1996): 1–18.

Kidd, D. A. "The Unity of Catullus 51." *Journal of the Australasian Universities Language and Literature Association* 20 (1963): 298–308.

Kinsey, T. E. "Catullus 51." *Latomus* 33 (1974): 372–78.

Miller, P. A. "Sappho 31 and Catullus 51: The Dialogism of Lyric." *Arethusa* 21 (1993): 183–99.

Newman, J. K. "Comic Elements in Catullus 51." *Illinois Classical Studies* 8 (1983): 33–36.

O'Higgins, D. "Sappho's Splintered Tongue: Silence in Sappho 31 and Catullus 51." *American Journal of Philology* 111 (1990): 156–67.

Rankin (see Poem 43).

Thom, Sjarlene. "Confrontation with Reality in Catullus 51." *Akroterion* 40 (1995): 80–86.

Vine, Brent. "On the 'Missing' Fourth Stanza of Catullus 51." *Harvard Studies in Classical Philology* 94 (1992): 251–61.

Wills, G. "Sappho 31 and Catullus 51." *Greek Roman and Byzantine Studies* 8 (1967): 167–97.

Poem 60

Weinreich, O. "Catullus c. 60." *Hermes* 87 (1959): 76–90. (in German)

Poem 64

DeBrohun, Jeri. "Ariadne and the whirlwind of fate: figures of confusion in Catullus 64.149–57." *Classical Philology* 94 (1999): 419–30.

Faber, Riemer. "*Vestis...variata*" (Catullus 64, 50–51) and the Language of Poetic Description." *Mnemosyne* 51 (1998): 210–15.

Konstan, David. *Catullus' Indictment of Rome: The Meaning of C.64.* Amsterdam: Hakkert, 1977.

Putnam, M. C. J. "The Art of C. 64." *Harvard Studies in Classical Philology* 65 (1961): 166–205. (Reprinted in Putnam, *Essays.* Cf. book section of this bibliography.)

Tathan, Gail. "Ariadne's *mitra*: a note on Catullus 64.1–4." *Classical Quarterly* 40 (1990): 560–61.

Thomas, Richard. "Callimachus, the *Victoria Berenices*, and Roman Poetry." *Classical Quarterly* 33: 92–113.

Poem 65

Block, E. "Carmen 65 and the arrangement of Catullus' poetry." *Ramus* 13 (1984): 48–59.

Lausen, S. "The Apple of C. 65: A Love Pledge of Callimachus." *Classica et Mediaevalia* 40 (1989): 161–69.

Van Sickle, John. "About Form and Feeling in C. 65." *Transactions and Proceedings of the American Philological Association* 99 (1968): 487–508.

Poem 68

Fear, T. "*Veronae Turpe, Catulle, Esse.*" *Illinois Classical Studies* 17 (1992): 246–63.

Forsyth, P. "*Muneraque et Musarum hinc petis et Veneris.* Catullus 68A.10." *Classical World* 80 (1987): 177–80.

Hubbard, T. "C. 68. The Text as Self-Demystification." *Arethusa* 17 (1984): 29–49.

Sarkissian, John. *Catullus 68: An Interpretation*. Leiden: Brill, 1983.

Simpson, Christopher. "Unnecessary homosexuality: the correspondent's request in Catullus 68A." *Latomus* 53 (1994): 564–69.

Poem 69

Noonan, J. D. "*Mala Bestia* in Catullus 69.7–8." *Classical World* 73 (1979): 156–64.

Pedrick, Victoria. "The abusive address and the audience in Catullan poems." *Helios* 20 (1993): 173–96.

Poem 70

Miller, Paul Allen. "Catullus c. 70: a Poem and its Hypothesis." *Helios* 15 (1988): 127–32.

Poem 72

Akbar Khan, H. "A Note on the Expression *solum...nosse* in Catullus." *Classical Philology* 62 (1967): 34–37.

Davis, J. T. "Poetic Counterpoint: Catullus 72." *American Journal of Philology* 92 (1971): 196–201.

Kubiak, D. P. "Time and Traditional Diction in Catullus 72." In *Collection Latomus: Studies in Latin Literature and Roman History* 4, ed., C. Deroux. Brussels: Latomus, 1986: 259–64.

Poem 76

Dyson (see Poem 8).

Moritz, L. A. "Difficile est longum subito deponere amorem." *Greece and Rome* 15 (1968): 53–58.

Powell, J. G. F. "Two Notes on Catullus." *Classical Quarterly* 40 (1990): 199–206.

Skinner, Marilyn B. "Disease Imagery in Catullus 76.17–26." *Classical Philology* 82 (1987): 230–33.

Poem 77

Arkins, Brian. "Caelius and Rufus in Catullus." *Philologus* 127 (1983): 306–11.

Pedrick (see Poem 69).

Poem 84

Baker, R. J., and B. A. Marshall. "The Aspirations of Q. Arrius." *Historia* 24 (1975): 220–31.

Levin, D. N. "Arrius and His Uncle." *Latomus* 32 (1973): 587–94.

Ramage, E. S. "Note on Catullus' Arrius." *Classical Philology* 54 (1959): 44–45.

Vandiver, Elizabeth. "Sound Patterns in Catullus 84." *Classical Journal* 85 (1989–90): 337–40.

Poem 85

Bishop, J. D. "Catullus 85: Structure, Hellenistic Parallels, and the Topos." *Latomus* 30 (1971): 633–42.

Poem 86

Papanghelis, T. D. "Catullus and Callimachus on Large Women: a Reconsideration of c. 86." *Mnemosyne* 44 (1991): 372–86.

Rankin (see Poem 34).

Poem 87

Copley, F. O. "Emotional Conflict and Its Significance in the Lesbia Poems." *American Journal of Philology* 70 (1949): 22–40.

Poem 96

Davis, J. T. "Quo desiderio: The Structure of Catullus 96." *Hermes* 99 (1971): 297–302.

Poem 101

Bright (see Poem 11).

Cederstrom, E. "Catullus' Last Gift to his Brother (c. 101)." *Classical World* 75 (1981): 117–18.

Howe, N. P. "The 'Terce Muse' of Catullus 101." *Classical Philology* 69 (1974): 274–76.

Robinson, C. E. "Multas per gentes." *Greece and Rome* 12 (1965): 62–63.

Poem 109

Thomson, D. F. S. "Catullus 107.3–4 and 109.1–2." *Liverpool Classical Monthly* 9 (1984): 119–20.

Poem 116

Forsyth, P. "Comments on C. 116." *Classical Quarterly* 27 (1977): 352–53.

Macleod, C. W. "C. 116." *Classical Quarterly* 23 (1973): 304–09.

Németh, B. "To the Evaluation of C. 116." *Acta Classica (Debrecen)* 13 (1977): 23–31.